THE VERY HUNGRY CELIAC

MELANIE
PERSSON

THE
VERY
HUNGRY
CELIAC

Your favorite foods made
GLUTEN-FREE

Hardie Grant

BOOKS

Contents

Introduction

Food has played a key role in my life for as long as I can remember. It's always been intrinsically linked with family, culture, friendships, travel – everything that has been important to me since I was really young. If you've picked up this book, chances are that your relationship with food has been affected by an intolerance, allergy or disease that has drastically altered your lifestyle (or the life of a loved one). While I admit that needing to avoid gluten constitutes a significant change, it's my goal to share with you the many ways that we can continue to enjoy good food. And by that I don't mean food that is just *good enough*, considering it's gluten-free. I mean food that will make you and your family and friends say, 'I can't *believe* this is gluten-free,' or better yet, it just won't be mentioned at all!

This book contains dozens of my recipes that I consider *surprisingly* gluten-free. This is food that I want to be enjoyed not only by people who have to avoid gluten but also by the people who you want to share the experience of food with. After all, I love to cook for people, but almost none of my friends are gluten-free, and I'm certainly not going to cook them food I can't eat and enjoy myself! So ultimately, the idea of cooking good gluten-free food to share with your loved ones has been the driving inspiration behind all of my cooking experience.

Most of the recipes I've included are for food that I grew up eating and enjoying and have found myself sorely missing in the years since my celiac disease diagnosis. Since I started sharing my recipes on social media and then later through the TV screen on *MasterChef*, the sheer number of people who have reached out to me describing how they lost their love of food and cooking as a result of their restrictions has really broken my heart. I hope this book can open your eyes to the gluten-free possibilities out there and maybe even fill a void with some of the food you've been missing.

To better describe the food included in this book, I need to explain a little about who I am as a cook and how I got here. When I was two years old, my family moved to Japan. We lived there for three years before returning to Australia, and I've continued to have a strong connection to Japan all my life. I was very privileged in that we travelled back often, maintained friendships, and I did two school exchanges there that helped me remember the language and keep me connected to the country I still consider to be my first home. After all, most of my earliest memories are from Japan, of my school and friends there, and, of course, the food that is a huge part of Japanese culture.

I finished high school in the south-west of Western Australia, not far from the famous Margaret River region. I was then chosen for an exchange program that sent me to Italy for a year, the purpose of which was to be immersed in the language and culture, which of course included food! I lived in Milan, made many amazing friends, had incredibly loving host families, and fell head over heels for everything about Italian cooking. I was in awe of this culture of cooking as a family unit, passing recipes down over generations, and cooking with simple, beautiful ingredients treated with the utmost respect. I came home to Australia and almost immediately found work in an Italian restaurant so that I could maintain this connection to Italy and, above all, keep learning.

At the heart of my passion for cooking is my love of learning, a fundamental part of who I am. I've been a student my entire life, moving through university to where I am now – a PhD candidate juggling academic research with a desire to cook, and to cook *constantly*. These pursuits might not be obviously linked, but it always made sense to me that I'd want to apply my desire to learn to my love for food, which is how I taught myself to cook in the first place. When I was diagnosed with celiac disease, the need for this application became even more apparent. Because really, it felt like a rug had been cruelly yanked out from under me. Being told that I had to give up gluten, which I knew was included in lots of Japanese and Italian food (two fairly 'gluten-heavy' cuisines), was frankly devastating, and for a while, I felt utterly defeated. That is, until my inner (highly competitive) student instincts kicked in.

I decided that settling for living without was not an option. Similarly, settling for 'good for gluten-free' food was not an option. I missed noodles, fresh pasta, soft bread and, above all, dumplings (which have been my favorite food for as long as I can remember). Of course, the commercially available options are improving all the time, and these are leaps and bounds better than what was available when I was diagnosed. But still, there is this assumption that we, as gluten-free people by necessity, will happily settle for less than completely delicious, a notion I simply refuse to accept.

So in saying all of this, please explore my recipes. At times they're simple and at times they can be quite complex, but always bear in mind that where recipes are difficult or require ingredients you might not have encountered before, I have done so with the goal of creating truly delicious food that *happens* to be gluten-free, which sometimes requires new techniques or strange ingredients. It is also worth noting that I have not set out to create a healthy recipe book or a beginners' recipe book. The fact is that these recipes are born from extensive research and trialling, and creating food that can compete with the gluten-containing versions is not always a simple task. I have tried to make them as accessible as possible, though, and encourage you to take the time to practise some techniques where necessary, as the results *will* be worth the effort, I promise.

On that note, I'll leave you to it! I very much hope you enjoy cooking, eating and sharing the food I've created here.

Love,
Mel

A Note on Health and Other Allergens

Books that focus on gluten-free food as a means to improve general health are plentiful. I am grateful to those books as they have obviously been part of my cooking journey and taught me a lot, especially in the early years of my diagnosis. However, my focus is on the *enjoyment* of food. Of course, not all my recipes are 'bad' for you, or sweet, but I also haven't set out to make recipes that are 'healthy' because, let's be honest, sometimes you just want a custard doughnut. Or a sugary fingerbun. Or enough dumplings to feed a small army. And that's okay! I don't think that we should be deprived of indulgences purely because we are restricted to gluten-free food.

On a separate but related note, this book focuses on being gluten-free without simultaneously removing all other allergens. I know that many people who have to eat gluten-free food may also be restricted by allergies or intolerances to other foods, but I have deliberately not made this book about cutting out all allergens for the same reason I have avoided making it about healthy recipes. Those books exist. Those recipes are plentiful and easily accessible online. That's not to say I have ignored other intolerances completely: I have included a key in each recipe indicating the presence of allergens and notes where relevant indicating how a recipe might be altered to cater for some other restrictions. It is not possible, however, to do this for every recipe without compromising on flavor or texture, so please understand that some experimenting on your part might be necessary, as it's impossible for one person (me!) to cater for everyone, no matter how much I wish I could.

Pantry Staples

Soy Sauce

Gluten-free soy sauce is easily accessible these days and is often labelled gluten-free. My personal favorite is Kikkoman, but there are many alternatives out there. You can also look for tamari, which is more likely to be naturally gluten-free. It is slightly different due to the manufacturing process but yields a very similar flavor profile. Alternatively, for a soy-free version, coconut aminos is becoming more popular all the time and is usually readily available in health food shops. Bear in mind that while tamari and coconut aminos can give a *similar* result, the flavor and salt level do vary between brands and varieties, so substituting precisely in my recipes will likely change the end result. As such, be sure to taste-test and adjust seasonings as you go.

Dark Soy Sauce

Gluten-free dark soy sauce is harder to source than regular soy sauce, but it does exist. Dark soy is richer in color, with some sweet caramel notes. It is also a little more viscous. If you can find gluten-free kecap manis, a sweetened Indonesian variety of soy sauce, you can substitute that for dark soy, but you should reduce the amount of any added sugar as it is usually considerably sweeter than dark soy. You can also use regular soy sauce with a little extra added sugar, but the final product won't be as richly colored as if you use dark soy or kecap manis.

Oyster Sauce

Oyster sauce is slowly becoming more and more accessible. There are a variety of brands that now test and label their oyster sauce as gluten-free and more still that are gluten-free by ingredient. There are also alternative varieties for those with other allergies or dietary requirements, such as vegetarian oyster sauce or, more specifically, mushroom oyster sauce.

Fermented Beans

Many varieties of fermented beans are used to impart bucketloads of umami flavor to dishes from all over Asia. There are sweet or salty versions used in many different applications – think of things like mapo tofu, miso soup or Japanese natto as just a few examples. These can be harder to find as gluten-free by ingredient (I'm yet to find any that are labelled GF), but they do exist. Don't be shy about checking the ingredients list of every jar in your local Asian grocer and if you find some, just experiment by adding a small amount to a stir-fry or the marinade for meat to be fried.

Sake

Sake (like mirin, below) is a variety of rice wine used ubiquitously in Japanese cooking. Sake usually contains around 15 to 20 per cent alcohol, so I often think of it in terms of the use of cooking wine in western cuisine. There are nicer varieties designed for drinking and cheaper varieties used for cooking. Sake is normally naturally gluten-free but always check the label. It is a staple for broths, braising liquids and marinades.

Mirin

Mirin, like sake, is a rice wine, but a sweetened variety with a lower alcohol content. A lot of recipes call for both sake and mirin, so I consider them both a staple in my pantry. I have found that Japanese brands of mirin are usually gluten-free by ingredient, so I recommend hunting for it in an Asian grocer that is likely to carry a few different brands. One thing to note is that it is sometimes sweetened with glucose syrup derived from wheat, which, while gluten-free, will not be suitable for someone with a separate wheat allergy.

→

Mijiu

Mijiu is a Chinese rice wine I use instead of Shaoxing wine. While it is not as flavorful as Shaoxing, it does have a higher alcohol content than sake or mirin and therefore still provides the added depth of flavor that alcohol can bring out in sauces and marinades. It is not always gluten-free as it is often brewed with wheat. However, I have found it easier to find gluten-free mijiu (brewed with soy beans) than gluten-free Shaoxing. Note that it isn't labelled 'gluten-free' and is only gluten-free by ingredient, so if you're looking, be sure to check the label.

Dashi Powder

Dashi is the powdered form of a Japanese fish stock made from bonito flakes. It is another staple in many broths and sauces, which is why it is always in my pantry. It is absolutely key to unlocking the Japanese flavor profile you might have been missing and is something that many people don't realize can be safe, which is why I've included it here. I have found that the ingredients vary slightly by brand, and while one of the most ubiquitous brands is gluten-free by ingredient, the other most common variety contains wheat starch, meaning it is of course unsafe, so always be vigilant with label reading.

Gochujang

Gochujang is a spicy fermented condiment used a lot in Korean cooking. Perhaps surprisingly, the majority of commercially available gochujang varieties do contain wheat. However, there are a couple of safe brands that are either gluten-free by ingredient or labelled gluten-free. I find gochujang to be a delicious way to add a level of spice and savory complexity that can't be achieved with chilli alone. I highly recommend trying it in a soup or stir-fry, or adding it to a delectable sauce to smother on chicken wings.

Chicken Powder

Chicken powder, or chicken bouillon powder, is a stock powder that differs slightly from what you find in the major supermarket chains. It's a common flavor booster used in Asian cooking but is not always gluten-free, so be sure to check the label. It often contains a small amount of monosodium glutamate, the naturally occurring flavor enhancer behind the taste of umami, most commonly known as MSG.

Rice Vinegars

In the same way that apple cider vinegar or sherry vinegar are staples in western cooking, rice vinegar varieties are often used to add flavor and acidity to many Asian dishes. White rice vinegar is gluten-free and easy to find in the supermarket, but black rice vinegar is much harder to find. It does exist, however, and is worth tracking down as it is a delicious accompaniment to dumplings or stir-fried vegetables.

Noodles

Noodles are something missed widely within the gluten-free community. Dry rice noodles are obviously a go-to option, but many don't realize the number of varieties available. Not only do the dried options go from vermicelli to wide ho fun noodles, there are also some varieties of Korean noodles that mix potato or cornstarch with the rice, making for a more substantial, chewier noodle. It is therefore worth checking the labels of noodles, even the ones that don't necessarily look like rice noodles. This goes for soba noodles, too, as traditionally these are made solely from the gluten-free grain buckwheat (although those noodles are harder to find). The fresh noodle selection in Asian grocers should also not be overlooked as some fresh rice noodle varieties are gluten-free by ingredient, and such noodles make for a really nice change to the shelf-stable versions. If you're sick of rice noodles altogether, you'll be excited to know that this book includes recipes for bouncy egg noodles *and* udon noodles, both of which are perfect for soups or stir-fries.

Xanthan Gum

Xanthan gum has gained attention over the last few years as a popular ingredient in gluten-free cooking and, as such, is now readily available in supermarkets and health food shops. This is due to the thickening and stabilizing properties it provides, which, in lieu of gluten, helps give elasticity and strength to gluten-free foods. Xanthan gum is added to recipes in this book in different ratios as different foods have varying needs for elasticity. For example, a light and airy cake requires less xanthan gum than a bread dough. So in the same way that 'normal' gluten-filled versions of these things would use low- and high-gluten flours, the gluten-free versions also vary in the need for additives to stabilize them. It should be noted that xanthan gum has a bitter, unpleasant taste if used in excess, so where stretchiness or flexibility is required in one of my recipes, I will always pair the use of xanthan gum with psyllium husk powder and/or a higher ratio of egg whites (occasionally egg white powder), both of which also help starches to bind.

Psyllium Husk Powder

Psyllium husk powder is another staple in gluten-free baking as it serves a similar purpose to xanthan gum. You can find it in most major supermarkets or health food shops (or ask them to order it in). When mixed with liquid, psyllium husks form a thick, viscous gel-like substance, and it is this property that is exploited in gluten-free cooking. Many gluten-free cooks prefer to use whole husks, which are ideal for loaves of bread or other large baked goods, but they can mar the silky texture of delicate foods like noodles, dumpling wrappers or filo pastry. Using whole husks also generally requires an additional step in the cooking process where the husks are first hydrated in water to produce the gel to be added to the other ingredients. I find that using powder renders this unnecessary as it can be mixed straight in with other dry ingredients and hydrated through the mixing or kneading process.

Note that psyllium husk powder may change the color of the product it's used in, usually adding a purplish-brown hue (a result of an antioxidant in the outer layer of the husk seed). This will not affect the taste or texture of your food, but it can be surprising, especially when making pasta or dumplings. If you are bothered by the color, you can try searching specifically for blond psyllium husk powder, but that can be tricky as it's not usually specified in the labelling. The simplest solution, if you have a high-powered blender or spice grinder, is to blend husks into a powder yourself. Just ensure that you mill the husks thoroughly to achieve a powdery consistency.

Neutral Oils

You'll notice some recipes call for a neutral oil, usually for shallow or deep frying. This simply means an oil with a neutral flavor such as vegetable, canola or rice bran oil. These have the additional benefit of having a high smoking point, meaning that they tolerate high heat during cooking.

Equipment Notes

Digital scales

Scales are essential for gluten-free baking and I highly recommend that you invest in a set of digital kitchen scales. Cooking and baking are sciences and, particularly in gluten-free recipes, there are many variables involved. Weighing ingredients will always give you the best, most consistent results, and make troubleshooting easier. Throughout this book, measurements larger than a tablespoon for dry ingredients are generally given in grams. You'll also notice that some recipes specify an approximate weight for the egg content required. This is because differing egg sizes can alter some recipes quite significantly. Use scales to measure eggs when specified by the recipe; when not specified, use standard large eggs. A bonus of digital scales is that they save on washing up – so it's a win-win!

Stand mixer or electric mixer

Many recipes in this book benefit from the use of a stand mixer, electric beaters or electric whisk. I always include instructions to mix by hand, but this often requires vigorous mixing for extended periods of time to achieve the right results. Please don't think I'm exaggerating the difference that thorough mixing can provide just because the recipe is devoid of the gluten that normally needs to be worked. I have found that both xanthan gum and psyllium husks (as well as some of the starches) are 'activated' in a manner similar to gluten.

Food processor

You might be surprised to know that many of the doughs made in this book are most easily made in a food processor. They are especially useful for using up scraps of dough, as kneading and bringing small pieces of rolled dough back together by hand is quite difficult. Simply place the scraps back into the food processor, add a few drops of hot or boiling water, and mix on high speed for a few seconds. The dough will be ready to use again.

Pasta rollers

As gluten-free products do not have the flexibility to stretch like 'normal' food, rolling by hand can be very tiresome because you need to apply consistent, gentle force, which takes time and care. Rolling by hand is of course possible, but it may take some practice (and patience) to achieve the incredibly thin result required for some recipes like Filo Pastry, for example (page 167). The easiest way to roll a lot of the doughs in this book is with a pasta roller, either the manual variety or the attachment for a stand mixer.

Thermometer

A digital thermometer is an incredibly handy gadget to have in the kitchen, particularly when you're moving from beginner to intermediate cook. I always include notes in my recipes about how to test a temperature if you don't have a thermometer, but they are never as accurate. It is likely that the results will still be good, but *if* something (in the more complex recipes) doesn't seem quite right, and all other instructions have been followed precisely, it's possible that some extra specificity in temperature testing may be required.

Oven

Note that the cooking times and temperatures listed in my recipes refer to a fan-forced oven. Conversions are easily found online. Be aware that many ovens have their own quirks, running a little hot or cold in some spots. If you're not familiar with your oven, an oven thermometer will help to ensure you're baking at the right temperatures.

Flour Blends

GF Starches and Flours

The alternative flours used in gluten-free baking can generally be broken down into two broad categories: starches (and finely milled flours that resemble starches) and high-protein flours. The most common of the former category are cornstarch, tapioca starch, potato and sweet potato starch, rice flour and glutinous rice flour (named for its glutinous properties and not to be confused with gluten). The higher protein flours come from grains such as buckwheat, brown rice, quinoa, sorghum or millet. Note that while oat flour is also a high-protein flour and popular for some gluten-free cooks, in Australia, those with celiac disease are generally advised to avoid oats unless they have undergone a medically supervised 'oats challenge' to ensure they do not react to avenin (the protein present in oat grains). I have found that I do have a slight reaction to oats and as such, do not cook with them at all, meaning they're not included in any of the recipes in this book. Other less commonly used flours pop up occasionally as their popularity in gluten-free cooking ebbs and flows (chickpea flour, green banana flour and hemp flour are some that come to mind).

As for the use of these starches and flours, no two gluten-free bakers use the same blend or have exactly the same preference for ratios. I find that the high-protein flours tend to make things dense, even gummy, while the starches are lighter and airier, and tend to lend themselves better to the binding properties of xanthan gum and psyllium husks. As such, I work almost exclusively with starches, recognizing that food made with these shouldn't dominate your diet but be consumed in balance, as with all other nutritional choices. While the high-protein flours are technically healthier, as I've described previously, I have not set out to make healthier food but rather food that is delicious and mimics the 'normal' gluten-filled varieties.

Using starches allows for baked goods to be light and airy and, depending on the cooking process and ratio of binders, also provides the stretch and chew ideal for bread products. Indeed, the Sweet White Bread Dough recipe I've included in this book (page 119) for use in all kinds of sweet and savory applications is the closest I've come to eating brioche or milk bread in the years since my celiac disease diagnosis.

Note that the starches used here should be white, finely ground and powdery. Cornstarch (or cornflour) comes in many varieties, including those used in Latin American cooking. The cornstarch I use is the powdery white starch, often used for thickening sauces or gravy (be aware that this is not always gluten-free, so be sure to check). Similarly, rice flour can cause some confusion as there are coarser varieties on the market; if it's too coarse, it will absorb water very differently, making recipes inaccurate. I have found that Asian grocers (local shops or online) are the best place to source the correct rice, tapioca and potato starches. They're also generally the most cost-effective choice.

Sweet potato starch (used in my Dumpling Flour Blend on page 11 and the Udon Noodles on page 61) can be a little tricky to track down. It can also be confusing because some brands use the labels of sweet potato 'starch', 'powder' and 'flour' interchangeably, while others differentiate between 'starch' (in reference to the powdery white form) and 'flour' (which is coarser and darker in color). The latter will not work properly, so be sure to use the white, starchy form. If you struggle to source sweet potato starch, you can use regular potato starch, which will still work well.

I have found that Asian grocers (local shops or online) are the best place to source the correct rice, tapioca and potato starches. They're also generally the most cost-effective choice.

Nut Flours

Flours made from ground-up nut varieties like almonds or hazelnuts have a place in gluten-free baking, but I tend to avoid using them too much simply because they're so common in gluten-free food. As much as I love a gooey flourless chocolate cake made with almond meal, or an orange and almond cake, these are easy-to-find gluten-free options that I know can be a little tiresome for the GF community. Similarly, cake recipes using almond meal to retain moisture in the cake (which is no doubt very effective) are quite common →

and accessible elsewhere, so I won't waste too much time doing the same here. I much prefer to use ground nuts in tarts and often switch between ground almonds, pistachios and hazelnuts to create layers based on ideal flavor pairings with the other tart ingredients.

My Basic Plain Flour Blend

Having described the many starches and flours taking up space in my pantry, I can turn finally to my preferred Basic Plain Flour Blend, the recipe for which can be found on page 11. This is a blend I use ubiquitously throughout this book and should therefore be the first thing you make before getting started. I make batches of 1–2 kg at a time and then use it like I would any other flour blend.

I know that the process of buying the individual starches can be daunting or seem overly complicated, but too often I have felt the frustration of finding what looks like an amazing gluten-free recipe only to discover that it can only be replicated with a specific flour that is not available to me. This is something I wanted to avoid in this book, and unfortunately, creating a flour blend from scratch is the only way to manage this.

Believe me, if there was a singular 'all-purpose gluten-free flour', I'd be the first to shout it from the rooftops (oh, how I wish there was!). The fact is that all blends vary in ratio, and all therefore function slightly differently, meaning that results are never consistent if different flours are being used based on accessibility.

Similarly, the unfortunate reality of gluten-free baking is the necessity of having many varied starches on hand. I *know* this is frustrating, especially if you're new to the process and are used to having one wheat flour that can be used for everything. Please believe that you will become used to this and get the hang of what flours are best for what purpose, and I hope that this book helps you get there.

With all that being said, I have tried (as much as possible) to make my flour blend versatile. If you'd like to try these recipes with a ready-made flour blend available to you, you may find it works perfectly. The easiest recipes to convert are generally those like cakes that rely heavily on the eggs and sugar for texture. However,

as it is impossible for me to test every recipe with every flour blend on the market, I can't vouch for the end result. What I *can* say is that *my* flour blend is designed to work with all these recipes (as well as many others), so it is well worth the extra initial effort. It should also be noted that in many recipes, my plain flour blend is paired with the use of some of the individual starches (noodles, pasta and dumplings, for example, should all be dusted with rice flour when being rolled and cut for best results), meaning that having the individual starches on hand is necessary anyway.

If cost-effectiveness is a concern for those making a blend for the first time, I'll point out that while the initial expenditure on individual ingredients might be slightly higher than simply buying a single flour blend, the cost per kilogram of my Basic Plain Flour Blend works out to be roughly the same as the supermarket home-brand blends, and significantly cheaper than the branded cup-for-cup varieties. The added bonus of making your own blend is, of course, that you then have the individual starches on hand for use when needed.

Basic Plain Flour Blend

Makes 1 kg (2 lb 3 oz)   DAIRY FREE   EGG FREE   NUT FREE   SOY FREE   VEGAN

This is the plain flour blend I have made to be used in most of the recipes in this book. I have found that it works as a good substitution for a lot of other recipes that aren't in this book too, so don't be worried about any going to waste. To convert this flour into a self-raising flour blend, simply add 5 g (⅛ oz) GF baking powder for every 100 g (3½ oz) of this mix. (This is best added as needed on the day of baking.) For information on GF starches and flours, see page 9.

315 g (11 oz) rice flour
250 g (9 oz) tapioca starch
250 g (9 oz) GF cornstarch
165 g (6 oz) potato starch
2 tbsp plus 1 tsp xanthan gum

1. Sift all ingredients together and mix until well combined. Sift and then stir a second time to ensure starches are evenly distributed. Store in an airtight container until ready to use.

Dumpling Flour Blend

Makes 1 kg (2 lb 3 oz)   DAIRY FREE   EGG FREE   NUT FREE   SOY FREE   VEGAN

If you make dumplings regularly (or plan to start), it is easiest to make a large batch of this flour blend to keep on hand. It really will make the process a lot less daunting, especially if you're new to the idea of using multiple flours in a single recipe.

300 g (10½ oz) glutinous rice flour
185 g (6½ oz) rice flour
185 g (6½ oz) sweet potato starch (see page 9)
295 g (10½ oz) tapioca starch
4 tbsp xanthan gum

1. Sift all ingredients together and mix until well combined. Sift and then stir a second time to ensure starches are evenly distributed. Store in an airtight container until ready to use.

Savory Favorites

The recipes in this section are mainly the odds and ends that can't be neatly categorized but which I also felt I had to include in my book. There are some light snacks here, like the Lavosh Crackers, as well as some of my all-time favorite meals like Katsu Curry. Many of these make great options for entertaining because there are components that can be made ahead of time and then reheated or cooked just before serving. I can guarantee the Ultimate 24-hour Karaage in particular is a total crowd-pleaser whether it's eaten hot or cold!

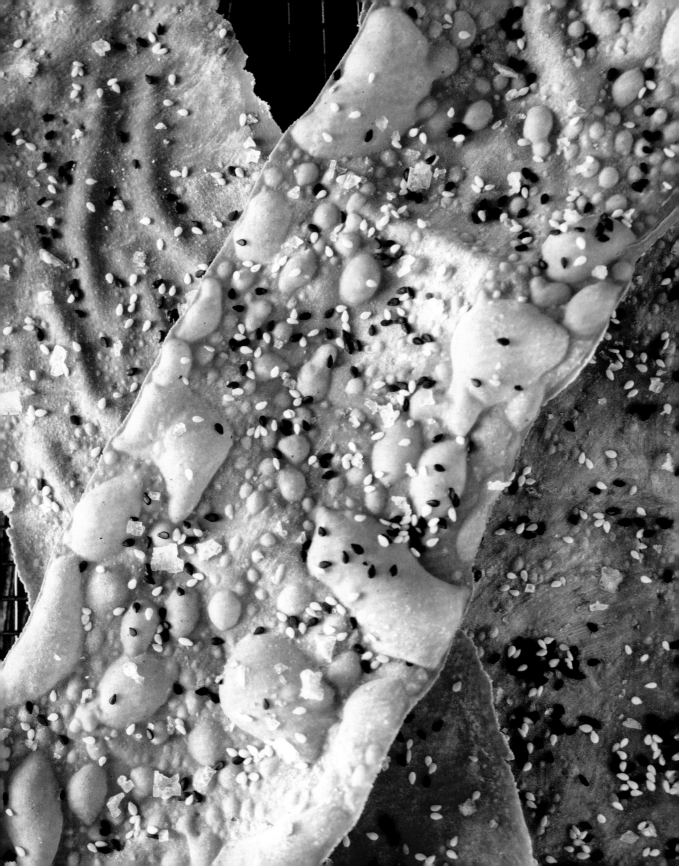

Lavosh Crackers

Serves 4–5

I haven't been able to find anything like lavosh crackers since my diagnosis, so I was very excited to make them successfully. I've opted to top these with a simple sprinkle of salt flakes and sesame seeds but you can absolutely get creative here. My Everything Bagels seasoning (page 117) would also be delicious on these.

60 ml (2 fl oz) warm water
½ tbsp caster (superfine) sugar
¼ tsp instant dried yeast
25 ml (¾ fl oz) olive oil
85 g (3 oz) Basic Plain Flour Blend (page 11)
1¼ tsp psyllium husk powder
½ tsp xanthan gum
⅛ tsp salt
1–2 tbsp olive oil, extra
1–2 tsp salt flakes, extra
1 tbsp white or black sesame seeds (optional)

1. Whisk together the warm water, sugar and yeast, then cover and set aside for 5 minutes while you prepare the other ingredients.

2. Combine the dry ingredients in a large bowl or the bowl of a stand mixer fitted with a paddle attachment.

3. When the yeast mixture has foamed, add the oil to it and whisk slightly.

4. Pour the yeast and oil mixture into the dry ingredients and mix on medium speed for 5–6 minutes. If mixing by hand, mix well with a sturdy spatula or wooden spoon, then knead by hand for 7–8 minutes. The dough needs to come together and be worked well to become smooth and pliable.

5. Lightly grease a fresh bowl with oil and scrape the dough into it, rolling the dough ball over a few times to coat it. Cover with plastic wrap, then a dish towel, and allow it to prove in a warm, draft-free area of your house for 30 minutes.

6. After proving, tip the dough onto a lightly floured surface and knead gently until smooth. Divide the dough into four pieces and cover with a dish towel.

7. Preheat the oven to 160°C (320°F) and line two large baking trays with baking paper.

8. Working on one portion of dough at a time, roll the dough out into a long sheet approximately 15 x 40 cm (6 x 16 in), dusting with flour as necessary, until it is less than 0.5 mm thick. This can also be done using a pasta roller taken to the thinnest setting. Once rolled, gently lay the sheet of dough on a baking tray.

9. Use a fork to prick all around the surface of the dough about 20 times to prevent it rising too much, then lightly brush the some of the extra olive oil over the dough.

10. Sprinkle the surface with salt flakes and sesame seeds if desired, then repeat with the other pieces of dough.

11. Bake for 12–14 minutes or until the dough is crisp and golden brown. Allow to cool, then store in an airtight container until serving.

Spring Rolls

Makes about 12

DAIRY FREE   EGG FREE   NUT FREE   VEGAN

Crispy fried spring rolls are, I think, universally adored, and they're something a lot of us miss. Not having access to commercially made spring roll wrappers is a disappointment, but it doesn't mean we need to miss out entirely. I make mine with a batter that gets brushed into a frying pan. The batter sets, leaving a pliable sheet of pastry that can be rolled and then fried to make a delectable snack. They're a little time-consuming but well worth it!

Wrappers

120 g (4 ½ oz) Basic Plain Flour Blend (page 11)

400 ml (13 ½ fl oz) water

¼ tsp salt

1 tbsp GF cornstarch, extra

1 tbsp water, extra

neutral oil, for frying

Filling

125 g (4 ½ oz) rice vermicelli noodles

1 carrot, grated or sliced into fine batons

1 garlic clove, minced

120 g (4 ½ oz) cabbage, shredded

1 spring onion (scallion), finely sliced

1 tbsp neutral oil

½ tsp sesame oil

1 ½ tsp GF soy sauce

¼ tsp white pepper

¼ tsp salt

¼ tsp caster (superfine) sugar

1. Start by making the batter for the spring roll wrappers. Weigh the flour into a large jug or bowl, add the water and salt and whisk well to combine. Pass the batter through a sieve or use a stick blender to remove any lumps, then set aside to rest for 30–40 minutes while you make the filling.

2. Place the noodles into a bowl of boiling water and leave to soften for 4–5 minutes.

3. Meanwhile, heat some neutral oil in a large pan or wok, then fry the carrot until just softened. Add the garlic and cook until fragrant, then add the cabbage. When softened, add the spring onion, then drain the noodles and add them to the pan. Toss well to combine.

4. Add the rest of the filling ingredients and continue cooking and tossing until the sauces are evenly distributed through the vegetables and noodles. Remove from the heat to cool while you finish making the spring roll wrappers.

5. Heat a large, flat-bottomed non-stick pan over medium-low heat without any oil. Whisk the batter to ensure it is smooth, then use a pastry brush to apply a thin layer of batter onto the dry pan, aiming for just over a 20 x 20 cm (8 x 8 in) square. It will start to cook as you brush so work reasonably quickly, making the layer as thin and even as possible (around 1–2 mm thick is ideal). After 4–5 minutes, the edges of the wrapper will start to lift away from the pan around the edges. The edges might be crisp, but most of the wrapper will be softer and a little sticky. Gently and carefully use your fingers (use heatproof gloves or some paper towel as a barrier if necessary) to peel the wrapper off the pan. Place the wrapper on a clean, flat surface, being careful not to fold it as it will stick to itself.

→

Repeat with the remaining batter, but do not stack the wrappers unless separated by baking paper or they will stick together.

6. Once you've used up all the batter, trim the wrappers (one at a time) on a chopping board with a sharp knife to form relatively uniform squares.

7. Position a wrapper with a corner pointed towards you and fold that corner towards the centre, overlapping the wrapper only by 2–3 cm (about 1 in) to create a straight edge. Place 1–2 tbsp of the spring roll filling along this edge, then lift the pastry edge up and over the filling. Roll once so the filling is sealed inside, then bring the left and right corners over the filling to seal the ends. Then roll towards the remaining corner. If the final corner doesn't adhere naturally to the spring roll to seal, create a slurry with the extra cornstarch and water. Stir and then dab that inside the end of the pastry like glue. Repeat with the rest of the wrappers.

8. Heat about 10 cm (4 in) of oil in a saucepan for deep-frying over medium-high heat. The oil is ready when a wooden spoon or chopstick sizzles when the end is dipped in. Fry the spring rolls until they are crisp and golden brown, then allow them to drain slightly on a cooling rack or sheet of paper towel.

9. Serve fresh and hot with your desired dipping sauce – sweet chilli is a personal favorite!

Ultimate 24-hour Karaage

Serves 4

Karaage or tori karaage is a type of Japanese fried chicken. This is a childhood favorite of mine that has become increasingly available and popular in Australia in the last ten years or so. Unfortunately, while the fried coating is naturally gluten-free (being made from potato starch), the chicken itself is usually marinated in soy sauce, meaning that restaurant-made karaage is rarely safe. On the plus side, this makes it a dish that is very easy to convert to gluten-free. My little trick that makes this chicken extra special, though, is to dredge the marinated chicken in the starch well before frying. This allows the starch to hydrate and produces an *incredible* crunchy coating without the need to double or triple fry. The only downside to this is that it requires some forward planning, because between the marinating and the hydration of the coating, this is best started the day before serving. Hence the name 24-hour karaage!

4–5 boneless chicken thigh fillets, skin on
3–4 cm (1 ½ in) piece of ginger, finely grated
3 garlic cloves, minced
3 tbsp GF soy sauce
2 tbsp sake
1 tbsp caster (superfine) sugar
½ tsp salt
250 g (9 oz) potato starch
neutral oil, for frying
Japanese mayonnaise and lemon wedges, to serve

1. Chop the chicken thighs into 4–5 cm (1½–2 in) chunks, keeping the skin as intact as possible, then place in a large mixing bowl.

2. Place the ginger, garlic, soy sauce, sake, sugar and salt into the bowl. Mix well, then cover and refrigerate for 12 hours or overnight.

3. After marinating, move the chicken into a bowl containing the potato starch then toss to coat well. This can be made easier by putting the starch in a ziplock bag then coating six or seven pieces at once by shaking them inside the bag.

4. When the chicken pieces are coated, pile them onto a plate, cover with plastic wrap and refrigerate for another 8–12 hours. This is an unusual step, and the chicken will stick together as the starch hydrates, but this results in ridiculously crunchy chicken after frying!

5. Once ready to cook, heat about 10 cm (4 in) of oil for deep-frying in a saucepan over medium-high heat. The oil is ready when the end of a wooden spoon or chopstick sizzles when dipped in.

6. Working in batches of six to eight pieces of chicken so as not to overcrowd the pan, carefully drop the chicken in the oil. Leave untouched as they become golden, then turn the pieces to ensure they're cooking evenly.

7. Fry for 3–4 minutes until the chicken is cooked through, then transfer to a cooling rack to drain off any excess oil.

8. Repeat with the rest of the chicken and serve with Japanese mayonnaise, lemon wedges or other condiments as desired (I love sweet chilli sauce).

Beer-battered Prawns

Serves 2–3

I could have battered fish here for a classic fish and chip recipe (and this recipe does work beautifully with fish), but I actually prefer other menu items when indulging at a fish and chip shop, so here are some battered prawns for a nice change of scene! Whatever you choose to fry, this batter is light and crisp, and it doesn't retain excess oil. It also colors quite nicely, unlike many gluten-free batters that retain a stubbornly white appearance.

50 g (1¾ oz) rice flour
100 g (3½ oz) GF cornstarch
½ tsp salt
¼ tsp GF baking powder
150 ml (5 fl oz) cold GF beer
neutral oil, for frying
300 g (10½ oz) raw, deveined prawns (shrimp), peeled with tail on

1. In a large saucepan or deep-fryer, prepare the neutral oil for frying over medium-high heat.

2. Prepare your prawns. I like to make a few small cuts into the underside of each prawn to straighten it out a little, then make a longer incision on the other side where it has been deveined, butterflying it slightly. This provides more surface area for the batter to cling to, resulting in a crunchier prawn. Place the prepared prawns on some paper towel, pat them dry and set aside while you make the batter.

3. Place the dry ingredients into a medium mixing bowl and whisk to combine.

4. When the oil is nearly ready (the end of a wooden spoon or chopstick sizzles when dipped in), create a well in the centre of the starch mixture and add the cold beer. Whisk until the batter is smooth.

5. Holding the prawns by the tail, dip them into the batter. Allow some of the excess to drip off, then carefully transfer to the hot oil.

6. Move the prawns around a little in the fryer to ensure they cook evenly. Cook for about 2 minutes before cutting one open to check for doneness.

7. Transfer the cooked prawns to a cooling rack to allow any excess oil to drain, then serve while still very hot.

Spanakopita

Serves 4

NUT FREE   SOY FREE   VEGETARIAN

Spanakopita isn't something I ate a lot of prior to being gluten-free, but it is something I got *many* requests for once I shared that I was working on a gluten-free filo pastry recipe. As I have never found a GF version to taste, and because so many recipes out there claim to be the ultimate or traditional version, I deliberately kept the filling for mine very simple to encourage you to change it up according to your preferences. The beauty of this recipe lies in the filo pastry, which can be rolled incredibly thin to mimic the one thing all spanakopitas have in common – flaky, crunchy layers!

1 tbsp extra-virgin olive oil
2 small brown onions, diced
2 garlic cloves, finely chopped
500 g (1 lb 2 oz) baby spinach
250 g (9 oz) Greek feta
1 tsp parsley, finely chopped
1 tsp lemon zest
1 extra-large egg
¼ tsp salt
⅛ tsp cracked pepper
1 portion of Filo Pastry (page 167)
3–4 tbsp extra-virgin olive oil, extra
1 tsp white or black sesame seeds (optional)

1. Add the olive oil to a large frying pan over medium heat and fry the onions and garlic. When translucent, remove from the heat and add the spinach, tossing the leaves through the onions until just wilted.

2. Transfer the wilted spinach mixture to a mixing bowl. Crumble in the feta, add the parsley and lemon zest, then stir to combine.

3. Crack the egg into the mixture and mix well. Season with the salt and pepper.

4. Lay out a sheet of filo pastry horizontally on a clean work surface. Brush off any excess flour, then sparingly brush some of the extra oil over the sheet of dough.

5. Take a portion of the spinach mixture and arrange it along the bottom edge in a thin log spanning the length of the filo sheet.

6. Starting from the bottom edge closest to you, roll the pastry over the spinach mixture, then roll it up all the way to the far edge of the filo sheet. Once you have a long thin log of pastry full of the spinach mixture, roll it in on itself in a spiral shape as it lays flat on the work surface.

7. Lightly oil a large round oven-safe dish or frying pan, then place the initial small spiral of spanakopita in the centre of the pan.

8. At this stage, preheat the oven to 180°C (360°F), then continue with the remaining sheets of filo and spinach mixture. Coil each completed log around the initial spiral in the baking pan. The logs should be snugly fitted together.

9. When you've finished this process, lightly brush the top of the spanakopita with olive oil, sprinkle with sesame seeds if desired, and transfer to the hot oven.

10. Bake for 60–75 minutes, or until the pastry is crisp and a deep golden color.

11. Serve while hot or, if keeping, allow to cool completely before storing in an airtight container in the fridge.

Gyūdon

Serves 3–4

Another childhood favorite of mine, gyūdon is a Japanese dish oozing with flavor and comforting warmth. It consists of thinly shaved beef and sliced onions cooked in a sweet soy-based liquid. This is then doled onto a large bowl of rice that soaks up all that flavor to become the ultimate comfort food. Topping this with an onsen egg isn't strictly necessary, but it's highly recommended to add even more richness. The meat used in this dish is generally very finely shaved beef. This is widely available in Asian grocery stores; otherwise your local butcher might be able to supply it.

5 g (⅛ oz) GF dashi stock powder

250 ml (8½ fl oz) boiling water

2 tbsp sake

2 tbsp GF mirin

3½ tbsp GF soy sauce

3½ tbsp caster (superfine) sugar

2 tbsp neutral oil

2 large brown onions, sliced

2 garlic cloves, finely chopped

450 g (1 lb) finely sliced or shaved beef brisket

steamed rice, to serve

spring onion (scallion), pickled ginger and
    sesame seeds, to serve (optional)

4 onsen eggs (optional)

1. Prepare the soup stock by mixing the dashi stock powder with the boiling water. Add the sake, mirin, soy sauce and sugar, mix and set it aside.

2. Heat the oil in a medium to large saucepan and add the onions and garlic. Fry until fragrant, then add the meat, separating it as much as possible as you add it to the pan.

3. Cook the meat, tossing it gently until lightly browned, then add the soup stock. Place a lid on the pot and allow to simmer gently for 35–40 minutes.

4. While the gyūdon is cooking, prepare the accompaniments. Cook the rice and finely slice the spring onion. If desired, prepare the onsen eggs.

5. After 35–40 minutes, the meat should be juicy and tender. Place a serving of steamed rice in a deep bowl, then add a generous portion of gyūdon. Top with spring onion, a sprinkle of sesame seeds, pickled ginger and an onsen egg if desired. Serve while hot.

Onsen eggs

Onsen eggs are a type of soft-boiled egg often served in Japan. The yolk is jammy while the egg whites are *just* set. They're a little fiddly to make but they go very well with gyūdon and other Japanese dishes like udon. The trick is to cook the eggs low and slow. While this is made easier with a sous vide machine or other temperature-controlling appliance like a Thermomix if you have one, it can be done with just a thermometer and standard kitchen equipment.

1. Prepare a pot or kettle of boiling water. Place room-temperature eggs in a heatproof jug and place the probe of a thermometer in with the eggs.

2. Fill one-third of the jug with tap water, then add boiling water until the thermometer reads between 65°C and 70°C (150°F and 160°F). Set a timer for 20 minutes, then check on the thermometer every 1–2 minutes to ensure that the temperature remains consistent.

3. Adjust water temperature by adding more boiling water when the temperature reaches 65°C (150°F), and tip water out of the jug as necessary to make room for extra boiling water.

4. After 20 minutes, remove the eggs from the water.

5. Tap each egg gently on a flat surface, hold it close to the base of a bowl so it isn't dropping from any height, then use your thumbs to pry the shell apart so that the egg plops out. The white of the egg should just be able to hold its shape but it will be very wobbly and soft.

6. Use a spoon to gently scoop the onsen egg onto your meal.

Spinach and Feta Gözleme

Makes 2

Gözleme is a type of Turkish flatbread, usually filled with a mix of spiced meat or vegetables. It is not typically a yeasted bread, but I have found that when working with gluten-free doughs, yeast helps to keep them light and adds a savory flavor that is so reminiscent of fresh warm bread. I have opted to keep the filling very simple here, using easily accessible ingredients in a vague attempt to make up for the fact that gluten-free doughs always require more ingredients than I would like. Of course, you can stuff these flatbreads with anything you fancy, so feel free to experiment with different vegetable or meat combinations. You could even sweeten these into a dessert with peanut butter or hazelnut spread with banana or strawberries!

Flatbread

90 g (3 oz) warm water

1 tsp caster (superfine) sugar

1 ⅓ tsp instant dried yeast

115 g (4 oz) Basic Plain Flour Blend (page 11)

1 ¾ tsp psyllium husk powder

⅓ tsp xanthan gum

½ tsp GF baking powder

¼ tsp salt

¾ tsp caster (superfine) sugar, extra

10 g (¼ oz) butter, at room temperature

rice flour, extra (to dust)

lemon wedges, to serve

Filling

½ brown onion, finely diced

1 garlic clove, finely chopped

2 tbsp extra-virgin olive oil

½ tsp cumin powder

½ tsp chilli flakes

¼ tsp paprika

¼ tsp salt

60 g (2 oz) baby spinach

90 g (3 oz) feta

1. Measure the warm water in a medium jug (warm water from the tap is fine – it should feel slightly cooler than bathwater, warm to the touch but not hot).

2. Add the sugar, then sprinkle in the yeast. Whisk it well, then cover with a dish towel and set aside somewhere warm (see Bread chapter introduction on page 103 for details) for 10 minutes.

3. Place the flour, psyllium husk, xanthan gum, baking powder, salt and extra sugar into a large bowl or the bowl of a stand mixer fitted with a paddle attachment. Stir to combine the dry ingredients.

4. After 10 minutes, the yeast mixture should have a layer of foam above the water (note that if it has not foamed, your proving environment is likely too cold or your yeast is no longer active). Tip this mixture into the dry ingredients and start mixing on medium speed. If you do not have an electric mixer, mix well with a wooden spoon.

5. When the majority of the dough is starting to come together (with some dry crumbs and pieces in the bottom of the bowl), scrape down the bowl and add the butter. Continue mixing for 4–5 minutes in a mixer or 6–7 minutes by hand. The dough should come together in a single ball, cleaning the sides of the bowl.

→

6. At this point, if using a mixer, increase the speed slightly and let it knead for 4–5 minutes, until the dough starts to get sticky again. Then lower the speed to medium-low and mix until part of the dough is sticking to the base of the mixing bowl. If mixing by hand, turn the dough onto a clean surface (do not dust with flour) and knead vigorously by hand for 6–7 minutes. The dough should get sticky again to the point that it is hard to handle as it clings to your fingers. Do not be tempted to add flour.

7. Lightly grease another medium-large bowl with oil, then gather the dough and place it in the bowl in one rough ball. Gently turn the dough over a few times to coat it lightly with oil on all sides. Cover with plastic wrap, then a dish towel, and leave to prove in a warm, draft-free place for one hour. While you wait, make the filling.

8. Add the oil, onion and garlic to a frying pan over medium heat. Fry, stirring until fragrant, then add the spices and salt. When the onion is translucent, add the spinach and toss it through the onion and spice mixture until the leaves have just wilted. Remove from the heat.

9. Allow to cool for 5–10 minutes, then crumble in the feta and toss to disperse it evenly through the spinach, onion and spices. Set aside.

10. After an hour, the dough should have doubled in size. Tip it onto a clean work surface and knead it by hand for about a minute until smooth and pliable. Divide the dough into two equal pieces. Working with one at a time, knead them gently, then roll them into neat balls by cupping your hand over the dough and moving in a circular motion against the work surface.

11. Once each ball of dough is neat and smooth, lightly dust the work surface with rice flour. Use a rolling pin to roll out the balls until they are 1–2 mm thick, dusting with more rice flour as necessary to prevent the dough from sticking to the rolling pin or the work surface. Roll them in as uniform a shape as possible to make filling and sealing them easier.

12. Once rolled, take half the spinach and feta mixture and spread it over one half of each dough sheet, leaving 1–2 cm (½–¾ in) of bare dough around the edge. Fold the empty half of the dough sheet over the filling and pinch the edges together, sealing the filling inside. Use a little water as glue if necessary to make the dough stick.

13. Fry the gözleme in a large, dry frying pan over medium heat until the underside is golden brown, then flip and repeat. Once cooked, slice into wedges or halves and serve with lemon if desired.

Katsu Curry

Serves 4

DAIRY FREE   NUT FREE

This was one of my favorite meals as a kid and something I longed for after I found out I had celiac disease. When cooking this at home, most people use the blocks of roux that you simply add to the meat, vegetables and cooking water to thicken it into a curry. Unfortunately, those ready-made sauce bases are prepared with wheat flour so are no longer an option. The good news is that you can buy Japanese curry powder made by one of the largest manufacturers of those curry bases and it's naturally gluten-free. This makes it possible to replicate the signature Japanese curry flavor at home. Look for the S&B curry powder in a small red tin at your local Asian grocer. You can use another curry powder for this recipe, and while it won't be quite the same, it will still be delicious.

The curry from this recipe can also be added to the Udon Noodles recipe on page 61 to make another classic Japanese favorite, curry udon (with or without the katsu). There is something incredibly satisfying about slurping thick, chewy noodles through the rich sauce.

Curry

- 3–4 medium potatoes, peeled and chopped into 3–4 cm (1 ½ in) pieces
- 2 large carrots, peeled and chopped slightly larger than the potatoes
- 1 L (34 fl oz) water
- 1 tbsp salt
- 2 large brown onions, peeled and quartered
- 1 GF beef stock cube
- 50 g (1 ¾ oz) butter
- 2 tbsp GF Japanese curry powder
- ½ tsp garam masala
- 3 tbsp GF cornstarch
- 1 tsp GF soy sauce
- 1 ½ tbsp caster (superfine) sugar

Tonkatsu (pork cutlet)

- 4 boneless pork cutlets
- 70 g (2 ½ oz) rice flour
- ½ tsp salt
- ¼ tsp white pepper
- 3 eggs
- 120 g (4 ½ oz) GF breadcrumbs (preferably homemade – see page 107)
- ½ tsp salt, extra
- neutral oil, for shallow frying
- steamed rice, to serve

1. Place the potatoes and carrots into a medium saucepan with the water and the salt, cover and bring to the boil. When the potatoes are half-cooked, add the onions and the stock cube, reduce the heat to low, cover once more, and cook until the vegetables are tender.

2. Meanwhile, make the roux for the curry by melting the butter in a small saucepan. Allow it to brown gently over low heat, stirring regularly, then add the curry powder and garam masala. Keep cooking over low heat, stirring constantly, until fragrant, then add the cornstarch, soy sauce and sugar. Combine into a thick paste, then remove from the heat.

3. Add the paste to the vegetables, stirring it into the liquid to ensure no clumps form. The water in the pot will thicken into a rich brown sauce. Set the curry aside while you prepare the katsu.

4. Use a meat mallet to lightly pound each pork cutlet on both sides until about 1 cm (½ in) thick. Set aside.

5. In a shallow bowl, combine the rice flour, salt and pepper. In another shallow bowl, crack and beat the eggs. In a third, combine the breadcrumbs with the extra salt.

→

6. One at a time, dredge each cutlet with flour,
   then dunk it into the beaten eggs. Finally, drop
   each cutlet into the bowl with the breadcrumbs
   and gently coat it before pressing it firmly into
   the crumbs. Flip the cutlet and repeat so that
   it is well crumbed on all sides.

7. Pour enough neutral oil into a large, deep pan to
   fill it 2–3 cm (about 1 in) deep. Heat it over medium
   heat while you finish crumbing the cutlets. The
   oil is hot enough to fry when the end of a wooden
   spoon or chopstick sizzles when dipped into it.
   Alternatively, drop a breadcrumb into the oil:
   if it floats to the surface and sizzles straight away,
   the oil is ready.

8. Gently lay the crumbed cutlets in the oil without
   overcrowding the pan. Fry for 2–3 minutes until the
   undersides are golden brown, then flip them over.

9. When both sides of the cutlets are golden brown,
   remove from the oil and place onto a cooling rack
   or some paper towel to allow any excess oil to
   drain away.

10. Slice the katsu and serve with steamed rice and
    a generous portion of curry.

Pasta and Gnocchi

One of the first things to understand for gluten-free pasta-making is that you will need to unlearn some of the principles of making regular pasta. Regular pasta hinges on the gluten – working it, resting it, hydrating it just the right amount. Gluten-free pasta will not act like normal pasta during the kneading, rolling and folding process, so it will be a matter of learning what this type of pasta should feel like and how to fix things if they go wrong.

If you have tried and failed at gluten-free pasta in the past, it's likely you tried to use a normal gluten-free 'plain flour' blend as a basic substitute for wheat flour. It was probably a brittle, dry mess that refused to come together during kneading or that broke apart time and time again as you attempted to roll it out. This is because a regular GF plain flour blend is a very poor substitute for wheat starch in the context of making anything requiring elasticity or pliability. To mimic the properties of gluten in a gluten-free flour, it is absolutely necessary to add ingredients that are going to transform the basic starch components into a workable dough. I have outlined key information for GF pasta-making in the numbered steps below, including some troubleshooting tips. I recommend you read these before taking on your first batch of homemade pasta.

1   Understanding binders

I think of my preferred binders as something of a holy trinity that I then tweak and manipulate depending on what I'm making. These magic ingredients are xanthan gum, psyllium husk powder and egg white. Generally speaking, I prefer to use all three in minimal quantities to achieve the best result. However, there are times when this is less appropriate, at which point one or two of the trinity can be used at a higher ratio to offset the lack of the third. Xanthan gum and psyllium husk powder have been discussed in more detail previously (see page 7), while the use of egg white is perhaps most relevant to pasta, noodles and dumplings.

The first thing to note is that I predominantly use whole eggs in gluten-free pasta instead of making a solely yolk-based dough. Using yolks as the only source of moisture content in a dough creates a beautifully yellow, rich pasta, but it necessitates a higher ratio of xanthan gum and psyllium husk powder (which then negatively affects the flavor). Working with gluten-free dough is a constant struggle against brittleness and breakage, so using this higher-fat, lower-protein option is exceedingly difficult. Using whole eggs and just one extra yolk means working with a higher protein content and less fat, which helps to bring the dough together and makes it much more workable.

2   The addition of oil

While adding oil to 'normal' fresh pasta tends to be based largely on personal preference, I consider it almost a necessity when making the gluten-free version. Gluten-free pasta requires a higher hydration percentage than regular dough because of its tendency to become brittle and break as soon as it starts to dry out. Adding just a small amount of olive oil to the dough with the eggs makes a fairly dramatic difference in preventing the pasta from drying out as quickly during the kneading and rolling process.

3   The need to knead

I have debunked elsewhere the misconception that gluten-free doughs do not need to be kneaded because of the lack of gluten. In my gluten-free recipes (and, in my experience, in GF recipes in general), xanthan gum and psyllium husks are both most effective when they have been worked, and worked quite vigorously. Conveniently, a food processor removes the difficulty associated with this.

Incorporating some heat into the dough during the kneading process – either through speed when using a mixer or via body warmth if kneading by hand – also positively affects the malleable properties of the starches in the Basic Plain Flour Blend. If you find, therefore, that the dough is remaining stubbornly brittle as you try to roll it, moisten your hands with a little warm water and then continue to knead for a few more minutes.

4   To rest or not to rest?

Resting wheat-based pasta dough (or indeed any wheat-based dough) is generally necessary to relax the gluten protein (as well as to hydrate the dough). When it comes to gluten-free dough, there is obviously no gluten needing to relax, but allowing it to sit and hydrate for 5–10 minutes is still beneficial. The risk in allowing it to rest is that the dough can dry out quickly and lose the warmth that kneading provided, which also helps with malleability. If allowed to sit uncovered, it can also very quickly develop a thin crust that is then difficult to reincorporate into the dough. I rest my dough in a ziplock bag, being careful to remove as much air as possible before sealing it closed.

5 Rolling (and dusting)

By hand

Once the dough has rested, divide the dough into two to make it easier to work with, leaving one portion in the resting container. Roll with a rolling pin into a roughly rectangular shape around 5 mm (¼ in) thick, avoiding incorporating any extra starch unless absolutely necessary. If the dough is fairly neat around the edges, it's a sign that it was well-kneaded, hydrated and contains enough moisture to proceed. If the dough is *very* rough around the edges, it means it has cracked rather than stretched as it's been rolled out. This is a sign that the dough either needs more kneading or a little more moisture. Before gathering it up to knead again, try moistening your fingers and running them all over the sheet of dough. Then fold the dough up, taking the shortest edges and folding them over themselves to create a short, thick rectangular shape once again. Rotate it 90 degrees so that the neat, folded edges are pointing straight ahead, then roll it out once more. Repeat if necessary, but if the dough doesn't improve after two attempts, it likely requires more kneading. Note that some roughness around the edges is expected as this dough will never be as pliable as regular pasta, but you should be able to roll it out to a thickness of 1–2 mm while still being able to lift and maneuver the pasta without it tearing.

On the opposite end of the spectrum, your pasta dough may be too moist. This is comparatively easier to remedy by simply rolling out the dough as thinly as possible before adding any starch. When it is unavoidable (if the dough is clinging to the rolling pin or your work surface), dust both sides of the pasta dough with a small amount of rice flour (this will be explained below) and spread it evenly over the surface of the dough. Then roll again. Continue to dust only as necessary until the pasta sheet is at the desired thickness of 1–2 mm. When finished, gently fold the sheet of pasta dough up and cover it with plastic wrap and a dish towel while you work on the second piece of dough.

With a pasta roller

Once the dough has rested, divide the dough into two to make it easier to work with. Begin rolling out one of the dough pieces with a rolling pin, leaving the other one in the resting container while you work. Roll it into a roughly rectangular shape about 1 cm (½ in) thick and approximately as wide as your pasta roller. If the dough is fairly neat around the edges, it's a sign that it was well-kneaded, hydrated and contains enough moisture to proceed. If the dough is very rough around the edges, it means it has cracked rather than stretched as it's been rolled out to this point. This is a sign that the dough either needs more kneading or a little more moisture. One of the benefits of a pasta roller is that the machine can help to knead the dough. Feed the pasta dough through the machine on the widest setting. If the dough holds together and is simply rolled into a thinner sheet, then adjust the width of the machine to a thinner setting and feed it through again. Once you reach the third or fourth setting, it will likely need a slight dusting with rice flour (this will be explained below) before continuing.

If the dough rips or tears, do not despair. This can happen if the dough is either too dry or too moist. Gather the pieces and roll them back into a rectangle, a little less thick than before, then pass it through again. If you can't easily push the dough back together by hand, it is too dry. Moisten your hands with warm water and knead for a few more minutes. Alternatively, if you're using a stand mixer, break up the dough with your fingers, moisten your hands and handle the small pieces of dough to transfer a small amount of water to the dough. Mix with a paddle beater attachment until the dough comes together (adding a little more moisture if necessary).

→

If the dough is clinging to the roller and coming through with pockmark-like indentations, your dough is too moist. Dust it with a light sprinkle of rice flour on both sides, swipe it evenly all over the dough, then pass it through again. If it tears, fold it up, roll with the pin, and pass it through again. This process will essentially help to knead the dough and bring it back together, so be patient. There is a definite learning curve with gluten-free pasta.

When the right moisture level is reached, the dough should handle easily and pass through the pasta roller without difficulty. You will likely still have to dust the dough sheet very lightly with rice flour as you reach the thinner settings on the pasta roller. Once the sheet is 1–2 mm thick, gently fold it up and cover with plastic wrap and a dish towel while you work on the second piece of dough.

Why rice flour?

As was briefly explained in the discussion of gluten-free bread flour blends (see page 9), a neutral flour like rice flour should always be used to dust any gluten-free food that will be cooked via boiling or steaming due to the presence of thickening gums such as xanthan gum in the main flour used for these foods. These gums have a very viscous quality when they come into contact with water, which is highly useful and necessary for making the dough pliable. And while having the gum *in* the dough does not affect the taste or mouthfeel (unless it has been used in excess), dusting flour that contains the gum onto the nearly finished uncooked product creates an unpleasantly slimy or slippery mouthfeel when it is cooked in water or in a moist environment. Using rice flour during the kneading and rolling process avoids this effect entirely.

6   Cooking

Gluten-free fresh pasta cooks very quickly. The cooking water should be well-seasoned with salt and be at a rolling boil over high heat when the pasta is added. If cooking spaghetti, fettucine or another long-stranded pasta variety, chopsticks or narrow tongs are the best implements to use to agitate the pasta while cooking to stop it from sticking together.

Depending on the thickness of the pasta, it should cook in 20–40 seconds. Be sure to agitate it 3–4 times while it is cooking. When the pasta floats to the surface, test for doneness. When it is cooked through, remove from the heat and drain immediately as overcooking will result in the pasta becoming gluggy and sticky. Transfer the pasta directly into your prepared sauce (off the heat) and toss gently to coat it evenly.

7   Storing

The pasta dough can be kneaded then stored airtight in the fridge for two or three days before rolling.

If storing already rolled or shaped pasta, dust a large tray or airtight container with rice flour. If it is long-stranded pasta, toss some rice flour through the strands as well and gather into loose bunches, coiling them up loosely but neatly. Arrange them on the tray or in the container, then seal and refrigerate for two to three days. Bunches of long pasta can also be frozen in ziplock bags for longer storage.

If storing smaller pieces like ravioli, dust with rice flour and spread them out as much as possible in the storage container, not exceeding about three layers of ravioli or the weight will cause them to stick together. Seal and refrigerate for two to three days. To store for longer, lay them in a single layer on a tray dusted with rice flour and freeze. Once frozen, transfer to a ziplock bag for easy long-term storage.

To cook pasta from the freezer, simply drop the frozen pasta directly into rapidly boiling water. Follow the cooking directions outlined above but cook for longer and allow the pasta to thaw in the water before you attempt to separate individual strands or pieces. Cook for 1–2 minutes, again testing for doneness when the pasta floats to the surface.

Pasta Dough

Serves 2–3

200 g (7 oz) Basic Plain Flour Blend (page 11)
1 tsp xanthan gum
1 ¼ tsp psyllium husk powder
⅛ tsp salt
3 extra-large eggs plus 1 yolk
    (about 180 g/6 ½ oz total)
1 tbsp olive oil
rice flour, extra

1. Place the dry ingredients (except rice flour) into a mixing bowl or the bowl of a food processor and mix to combine. A stand mixer fitted with a paddle attachment can also be used.

2. In a separate jug, whisk together the eggs and extra yolk (adding a little water if less than 180 g) with the olive oil.

3. Pour the egg and oil mixture into the dry ingredients and mix on medium speed until a dough forms. A rough crumb will develop first, and then as it comes together, it will begin to roll around the bowl of the food processor, leaving the sides clean. Continue mixing until the dough is smooth. If mixing by hand, combine well with a sturdy spatula or wooden spoon, then knead by hand for about 10 minutes. If the dough is still not smooth and pliable, kead or mix in a teaspoon of hot water at a time (boiling water if using a food processor) until it does. Divide the dough into two and work with one portion at a time, covering the other with plastic wrap to keep it from drying out.

4. If using a mechanical pasta roller, start by rolling the dough with a rolling pin until it is about 1 cm (½ in) thick, then feed it through the roller on the widest setting. Continue to feed it through the roller, reducing the width after each pass through. If the dough is tearing easily or crumbling along the edges, you may need to fold the sheet into a thicker rectangle and pass it through a wider setting. Going back and forth between the widest settings and slightly thinner settings and folding the dough back up between passes will help to work the dough and bring it together. If this is necessary, it's likely that the dough wasn't kneaded enough initially or is a little too dry. Once the dough is on the third or fourth setting, it may start warping as it passes through the machine as it sticks slightly. Dust lightly with rice flour as necessary to keep the dough smooth and silky.

5. To roll by hand, use a rolling pin to work the dough into a long, thin sheet, only dusting lightly with rice flour when necessary as the dough becomes thinner. Continue to move the dough around the work surface, flipping it over intermittently to prevent it from sticking.

6. Once the pasta has been rolled, cut or fold it as desired. To cut the pasta into spaghetti or ribbons for a wider pasta, dust the dough well with rice flour, then fold the shorter ends towards the centre of the sheet to create a sort of flat, thick log. Use a sharp knife to cut through the folded layers at the desired width. Alternatively, cut with a mechanical pasta cutter. The pasta can also be folded into ravioli if desired.

7. To cook the pasta, bring a large pot of water to the boil. Season it well with salt, then add the pasta, stirring gently to keep it from clumping together. Fresh pasta will cook in 20–40 seconds (maybe longer if the pasta is quite thick) while frozen pasta will cook in about a minute or two.

Gnocchi

Serves 4–5

EGG FREE NUT FREE SOY FREE VEGETARIAN

4–5 large royal blue potatoes
(or other potatoes good for mashing)
1 tbsp salt
80 g (2 ¾ oz) Basic Plain Flour Blend (page 11)
40 g (1 ½ oz) finely grated parmesan
½ tsp salt
⅛ tsp cracked black pepper
rice flour, to dust

1. Place the potatoes (whole, unpeeled) in a large saucepan and cover with water. Add the salt, then bring to a boil and cook for 35–40 minutes. A knife should be able to pass through a potato with little resistance.

2. Drain the potatoes and allow them to cool slightly before transferring them to the fridge to cool completely.

3. Once cooled, remove the skins from the potatoes – they should peel off very easily – and pass them through a potato ricer or food mill into a mixing bowl. They can also be mashed with a potato masher or fork but this will result in a denser gnocchi.

4. When you have 400 g (14 oz) of cold riced or mashed potato (reserve any excess potato for another meal or batch of gnocchi), add the flour, parmesan, salt and pepper. Stir the ingredients briefly with a fork or butter knife to combine, then tip onto a clean surface to work by hand.

5. Bring the ingredients together as a dough with a compressing and squashing movement. First place your hands on either side of the pile and push inwards. Then place your hands palm down on top of the pile and squash down. Rotate the pile and repeat. Continue this process, intermittently turning the pile over between squashing and rotating until it reaches a slightly sticky but smooth dough-like consistency.

6. Divide the dough roughly into six pieces. Work with one at a time, rolling the piece into a log about 2 cm (¾ in) in diameter. Once rolled, dust the log lightly in rice flour and cut at 2 cm (¾ in) intervals to create lots of smaller pieces of dough.

7. Roll these pieces individually over a gnocchi board or the tines of a fork to form the characteristic ridges around the outside of the gnocchi while leaving a small indent where your finger pressed into the dough (this will catch the sauce later). Repeat with the rest of the gnocchi dough. (Note that gnocchi dough stores well in the fridge if sealed in an airtight container and can be rolled up to three days after being made.)

8. To cook the gnocchi, bring a large pot of salted water to the boil. Add the gnocchi and stir gently to prevent them sticking. When they float to the surface, allow another 20–30 seconds before scooping them out with a slotted spoon or kitchen spider.

9. The gnocchi can be tossed directly into a sauce and served, or you can allow the cooked gnocchi to cool and dry a little, then fry them in a pan to crisp up slightly.

Prawn Spaghetti

Serves 2–3

Everyone has a go-to dish that is simple and quick enough to pull out on a lazy day but that is somehow also knock-you-over scrumptious. This is mine! Feel free to tweak it with your favorite herbs or to add other seafood or vegetables. Sometimes I'll add some fish or squid (or leave out the seafood altogether) or grated zucchini, and I'll often just make it with shop-bought pasta. But however you make it, this is bound to be delicious and very satisfying.

3 tbsp extra-virgin olive oil
4 garlic cloves, minced
1 long red chilli, finely sliced
1 roma or field tomato, diced
½ tsp cracked black pepper
200 g (7 oz) raw, peeled, deveined prawns (shrimp)
100 g (3½ oz) grape or cherry tomatoes
400 g (14 oz) fresh Pasta Dough, cut into spaghetti (see page 40)
3 tbsp flat-leaf (Italian) parsley, chopped (optional)

1. Bring a large pot of salted water to the boil.

2. Heat the oil in a large frying pan over medium heat, then add the garlic and chilli. Allow to cook for 1–2 minutes, stirring regularly, until fragrant. Add the diced tomato and cracked pepper, and continue to cook for 2–3 minutes until the tomato has broken down. Add a little of the salted pasta water to loosen if the tomato is sticking to the pan.

3. Raise the temperature to high heat, then add the prawns and the grape or cherry tomatoes. Cook the prawns for about 30 seconds on one side, then turn them over and continue to cook.

4. Add the fresh pasta to the boiling water and cook for about 30 seconds. Take about half a cup of pasta water out of the pot, add to the prawns and agitate the pan to create a sauce from the tomato and pasta water. Add the parsley to the pan.

5. Drain the pasta and add it to the frying pan. Turn off the heat and toss to coat all the spaghetti with the tomato sauce.

6. Serve immediately, topping with a little extra parsley if desired.

Double-stuffed Ravioli

Serves 3–4

I'm not going to lie to you, these are a bit of a project. They're very fun to make, though, and if you want to practise your pasta-making skills or have a day of pasta-making therapy, they're absolutely perfect. If you've got the time and energy you will be rewarded, because the flavor is divine. So good, in fact, that they don't normally make it into a sauce when I make them at home. My partner and I will start 'snacking' on them fresh from the boiling water, and before we know it, they're all gone! If you have more self-control, they're ideally paired with a light sauce like the brown butter and sage sauce used with the gnocchi on page 53 or a light tomato sauce that isn't going to overpower the delicate flavors.

400 g (14 oz) butternut pumpkin (winter squash), peeled and chopped
2–3 tbsp extra-virgin olive oil
¼ tsp salt
⅛ tsp cracked black pepper
1–2 sprigs fresh rosemary
1 small garlic bulb
1 portion of Pasta Dough (page 40)
240 g (8½ oz) ricotta
40 g (1½ oz) mascarpone
1 tsp lemon zest
¼ tsp salt, extra
⅛ tsp cracked black pepper, extra
rice flour, to dust

1. Preheat oven to 180°C (360°F). Spread the pumpkin on a large baking tray, then drizzle with some of the olive oil. Season the pumpkin with the salt and pepper, then add the sprigs of rosemary to the tray.

2. Trim the top off the garlic bulb and place it on a sheet of aluminium foil. Drizzle with a little of the olive oil and sprinkle with a little more salt and pepper. Wrap the aluminium around the bulb, then place it on the baking tray with the pumpkin.

3. Roast in the oven for 50–60 minutes until the pumpkin is tender. Meanwhile, make the Pasta Dough according to directions on page 40. Before rolling it out, seal it well to prevent it drying out, and make the ricotta filling.

4. In a small mixing bowl, combine the ricotta, mascarpone, lemon zest and extra salt and pepper. Transfer to a piping bag and set aside.

5. When the pumpkin is tender enough to eat with a spoon, transfer it to a food processor or the canister of a stick blender. Unwrap the garlic bulb and squeeze out three or four of the roasted cloves. Add that to the pumpkin, then blitz until smooth. Taste and adjust seasonings as necessary, then transfer the pumpkin filling to a second piping bag and set aside.

6. Roll out the pasta dough into sheets approximately 0.8 mm thick (dusting with rice flour as necessary). Cut the sheets into rectangular pieces approximately 6 x 12 cm (2½ x 4¾ in), then gather any scraps to roll and repeat, creating as many rectangular pieces as possible.

7. Seal the prepared pieces in plastic or an airtight container to keep them from drying out as you work. Once you have finished cutting the pasta, start to fill them with the two fillings.

8. Place a small rectangular piece of pasta horizontally in front of you. Pipe a small amount of ricotta in the middle of the left-hand side, leaving 1–2 cm (½–¾ in) on the left side and 1 cm (½ in) between the filling and the central line for sealing (see photos over page). Repeat on the right side with the pumpkin.

9. Use your finger to dab a little bit of water on the top half of the pasta around the piped lines of filling.

→

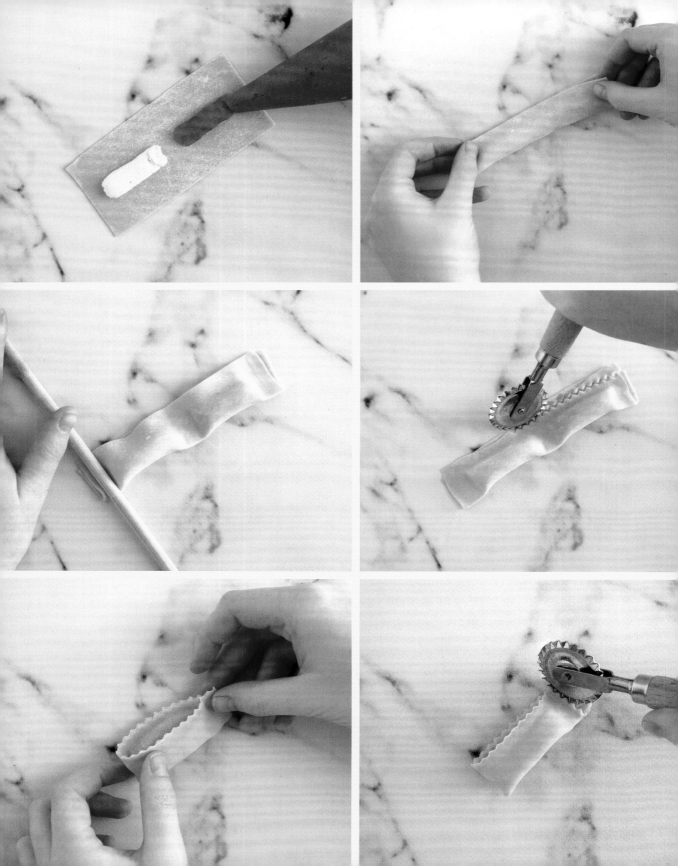

10. Take the edge of pasta closest to you and fold it over the filling, lining it up neatly with the furthest edge. Don't press down yet.

11. Use a pasta rod (you can use any narrow cylindrical instrument like a chopstick or straight metal straw) to press and roll the pasta together in a small rocking motion along the central vertical line, separating the two lines of filling piped inside.

12. Repeat on the left and right sides of the filling, pushing down close to the filling and rolling outwards, away from the filling. Where two seams of pasta are joining, the aim is the flatten them into the width of a single layer, so apply a little bit of pressure to do this. Some of the filling might squeeze out but that is okay.

13. Next, hold the rod horizontally and press the pasta down along the top edge above the fillings, sealing the top edges. Roll from the fillings outwards, away from you, until that seal is the thickness of a single layer of pasta. You should now have a narrower rectangle of pasta with two bulges of filling sealed inside. Be sure to seal well as the pasta will otherwise come apart during cooking or allow water to seep into the pockets of filling.

14. Trim along the top edge with a knife or, for a fluted effect, use a pasta cutter with a single-toothed blade.

15. Dab a little water along the right edge, then take the left half of the stuffed rectangle and fold it over the right half, lining up the left seam with the right.

16. Use the rod to join the seams together, pressing down as you roll outwards from the sealed fillings, again applying enough pressure to reduce the seam to the thickness of a single pasta layer.

17. Trim this new seam with the same method you used for the top seam. You should now have a bite-sized pillow of pasta with two separately encased pockets of filling.

18. Repeat with the rest of the pasta rectangles and filling. While doing multiple pieces of pasta at once is possible for experienced pasta-makers, I'd recommend most people work with one piece at a time, as gluten-free pasta dries faster than regular pasta, which can make folding difficult.

19. To cook, bring a large pot of salted water to a gentle boil. Cook the pasta for 50–60 seconds or until the pasta is tender.

20. Remove the pasta with a kitchen spider or slotted spoon, and toss with a simple sauce of your choice – I recommend brown butter and sage (see page 53) or a light and simple tomato-based sauce.

21. Serve fresh and hot. Alternatively, the uncooked folded pasta can be stored in the fridge (in a single layer) or freezer. If freezing, spread the pasta on a tray lightly dusted with rice flour and freeze. Once frozen, gather and keep in a ziplock bag or container. Then cook from frozen.

Mushroom Ravioli

Serves 5–6

NUT FREE   SOY FREE   VEGETARIAN

If you like mushrooms, you're sure to love this ravioli that *oozes* loads of mushroom flavor. The porcini mushroom soaking liquid creates a very rich sauce that just lightly coats the pasta, complementing the mushroom ravioli filling. I've kept this quite light because that's how I prefer my pasta, but if you wanted to make this more decadent, you could even add a little cream to the sauce, which would also be delicious.

2 portions of fresh Pasta Dough (page 40)
1 tbsp extra-virgin olive oil
1 shallot, finely diced
2 garlic cloves, minced
150 g (5 ½ oz) button mushrooms, sliced
¼ tsp salt
⅛ tsp cracked black pepper
30 g (1 oz) ricotta
small handful of parsley leaves
40 g (1 ½ oz) dried porcini mushrooms
700 ml (23 ½ fl oz) boiling water
rice flour, to dust
40 g (1 ½ oz) unsalted butter
parmesan cheese, to serve
extra parsley, to serve

1. Prepare the pasta dough according to directions on page 40. Before rolling the dough out into sheets, wrap it well in plastic and set it aside while you prepare the filling.

2. Heat the oil in a medium saucepan over medium heat, then add the shallot and garlic and fry until fragrant. Add the button mushrooms and season with salt and pepper.

3. Fry until the mushrooms are nicely brown and soft, then transfer the mushroom mixture to the bowl of a food processor. Add the ricotta and parsley leaves, then pulse until the mixture resembles a paste. Taste and adjust seasoning as required, then transfer to a piping bag.

4. Place the dried porcini mushrooms in a heatproof jug and add the boiling water. Let sit while you roll out the pasta and make the ravioli.

5. If rolling by hand, see steps 8 to 12. If using a pasta roller, roll the pasta out into four equal-length sheets to the sixth or seventh width setting (about 0.8 mm thick), dusting with a little rice flour only as necessary.

6. Pipe 2 cm (¾ in) blobs of the mushroom filling onto one sheet of pasta in two rows spaced 2–3 cm (about 1 in) apart. Wet a pastry brush with water and use it to *lightly* moisten the pasta around the blobs of filling, then quickly place a second sheet of pasta over the top. Use your fingers to smooth the pasta around the blobs of filling, but be gentle as GF pasta is not as flexible as regular pasta and won't stretch as easily.

7. Dust the pasta lightly with rice flour, then cut around the blobs of filling using a knife, ravioli stamp or cookie cutter. Set them aside and repeat with the other sheets of pasta dough. Once finished, prepare the pasta sauce (skip to step 13).

8. If rolling by hand, it is likely to be easier to roll the dough out into a single sheet. Get it as thin as you can, preferably slightly less than 1 mm thick. Rather than overlap one sheet over another separate sheet as you would if rolling with a pasta roller, you will fold half the pasta sheet over the other half to encase your filling. This will be easiest if you can keep the pasta sheet as uniform and symmetrical as possible. Dust with a little rice flour as necessary to prevent the pasta from sticking to the work surface or rolling pin.

9. Once you've rolled out the pasta sheet, pipe 2 cm (¾ in) blobs of the mushroom filling all over one half of the sheet, spaced 2–3 cm (about 1 in) apart.

→

10. Wet a pastry brush with water and use it to *lightly* moisten the pasta around the blobs of filling, then quickly fold the blank half of the pasta sheet over the half with the mushroom filling.

11. Use your fingers to smooth the pasta around the blobs of filling, but be gentle as GF pasta is not as flexible as regular pasta and won't stretch as easily.

12. Dust the pasta lightly with rice flour, then cut around the blobs of filling using a knife, ravioli stamp or cookie cutter and set them aside.

13. Place a large pot of salted water over high heat. While waiting for it to boil, strain the liquid from the porcini mushrooms into a medium saucepan over medium heat.

14. Bring the mushroom stock to a simmer and allow it to reduce by about two-thirds. Turn the heat to low, then add the butter and stir well to emulsify it with the stock. It should thicken and become glossy. Keep it warm over low heat.

15. When the salted water is boiling, add the ravioli and stir gently with a slotted spoon to stop them sticking. Cook for about a minute, then test for doneness. Drain when the pasta is tender, reserving some pasta water in case the mushroom sauce has thickened too much.

16. Toss the ravioli in the mushroom stock, adding a handful of the parmesan cheese to melt into the sauce. Adjust seasoning according to taste, then serve, topping with more parmesan and parsley as desired.

Gnocchi with Pumpkin and Sage

Serves 3–4

Pan-fried gnocchi makes for a nice change to the boiled gnocchi that is usually served in a rich sauce. Those dishes are fantastic and comforting, but I find them to be a little heavy to be eaten when it's not cold and rainy. Pan-frying the gnocchi creates some interesting textural differences and makes them perfect to be coated in a simple butter sauce. Add roasted pumpkin and some greens and you've transformed the gnocchi into a lighter dish that works all year round.

300 g (10 ½ oz) butternut pumpkin (winter squash), peeled and chopped
3 garlic cloves
2–3 tbsp olive oil
½ tsp salt
⅛ tsp cracked black pepper
20 g (¾ oz) pine nuts
80 g (2 ¾ oz) salted butter
7–8 sage leaves
1 portion of Gnocchi (page 41)
60 g (2 oz) rocket (arugula)
shaved parmesan, to serve

1. Preheat oven to 180°C (360°F). Spread the pumpkin on a baking tray with the garlic and toss with the olive oil, salt and pepper. Roast for 50–60 minutes or until the pumpkin is tender.

2. Place a large pot of salted water over high heat.

3. Place the pine nuts in a large frying pan over medium-low heat, tossing them gently until they brown slightly. Remove nuts and set aside.

4. Place the butter in the pan and allow it to melt, then reduce heat to low. Add the sage leaves. The butter will foam and slowly start to change color. When the butter has stopped foaming and has browned, remove it from the heat. The sage leaves should have crisped up in the butter.

5. When the water is at a rapid boil, add the gnocchi. Stir gently to prevent them sticking. When they float to the surface, allow another 20–30 seconds before scooping them out with a slotted spoon or kitchen spider and allowing them to cool a little on a plate. Space them out and dab away excess moisture with some paper towel.

6. Heat a large, clean, non-stick frying pan over medium-high heat, then add the gnocchi, spacing them evenly around the pan. Allow to fry for a minute or two, then turn them over. Cook until they have crispy, golden brown patches, then toss them through the brown butter and sage.

7. To serve, portion the gnocchi onto serving plates. Add pieces of roast pumpkin and the toasted pine nuts. Drizzle any excess brown butter over the plates, then top with the rocket and shaved parmesan. Season with more salt and cracked pepper to taste if necessary.

Gnocchi Fritti

It might seem like a lot of effort to make gnocchi from scratch just for a tasty snack, so I suggest you keep this option in mind for any leftover gnocchi you have from another meal. Deep-frying cooked gnocchi creates crispy pillows of potato that are tasty on their own, so serving them with parmesan, salt and pepper takes them to the next level – you won't want potato chips or fries when you can have cheesy fried gnocchi!

leftover Gnocchi (page 41)
neutral oil for frying
salt flakes and cracked black pepper, to taste
60 g (2 oz) parmesan, finely grated

1. Cook the gnocchi in a large pot of salted water at a low boil. Stir gently to prevent them from sticking. When they float to the surface, allow another 20–30 seconds before scooping them out with a slotted spoon or kitchen spider.

2. Spread the cooked gnocchi out on a clean tray to cool, then dab away excess moisture with a paper towel. Heat about 10 cm (4 in) of oil in a saucepan for deep-frying over medium-high heat. The oil is ready when the end of a wooden spoon or chopstick sizzles when dipped in.

3. Drop gnocchi individually into the oil in batches, spacing them out around the pan to prevent them from sticking.

4. When the gnocchi are golden brown and crisp, remove from the oil and leave to drain and cool slightly on a tray.

5. To serve, season generously with salt flakes and cracked pepper, then top with parmesan.

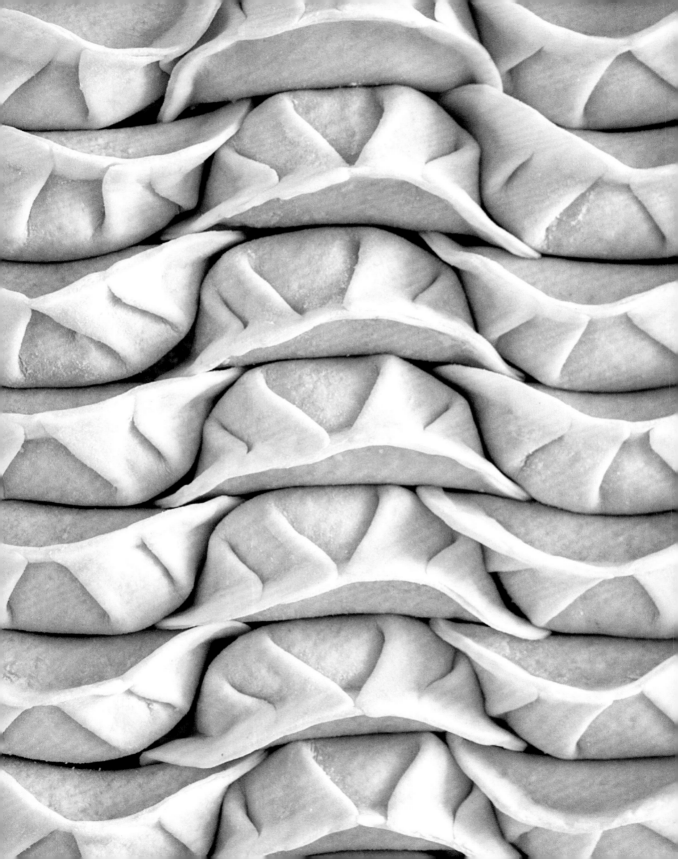

Noodles and Dumplings

The difficulties associated with making gluten-free noodles and dumpling wrappers largely overlap with those relating to gluten-free pasta or other thin doughs like filo pastry. Creating dough that is thin, stretchy and chewy, and that can be steamed, boiled or fried without the assistance of gluten is a tough nut to crack. However, once you start to understand the principles of binding gluten-free starches and get the feel for working with gluten-free doughs, it becomes a lot simpler.

This book includes two base recipes for noodles (springy egg noodles and udon noodles) and two base recipes for dumpling wrappers (one akin to wonton wrappers – thin, silky and delicate – and the other a little thicker and slightly chewy, perfect for a meatier mouthfeel). These recipes rely heavily on the same binding principles I have explained for the making of gluten-free pasta, so I'd highly recommend referring to those notes before you embark on making these. It should also be noted that the rolling, cutting and cooking methods of the noodles and wrappers vary slightly depending on the application, so follow the specific directions provided in each recipe.

Egg Noodles

My egg noodles are silky and springy, perfect for a number of applications including ramen or stir-fried dishes like chow mein. The dough differs from that of udon noodles and dumpling wrappers because of the addition of lye water or a lye water substitute (which should be made beforehand – see page 59). This enhances the yellow color and gives a bouncy mouthfeel not experienced with pasta or other similar egg-based noodles. Because of the higher ratio of egg yolk in these noodles, they contain psyllium husk powder to provide some extra stability and elasticity. The dough for these egg noodles should be rolled to approximately 1 mm thick then cut to the desired width either by hand or using a mechanical cutter (I prefer to cut these noodles very finely using an angel hair pasta-cutting tool).

100 g (3 ½ oz) rice flour
75 g (2 ¾ oz) GF cornstarch
75 g (2 ¾ oz) tapioca starch
50 g (1 ¾ oz) glutinous rice flour
4 tsp xanthan gum
3 ½ tsp psyllium husk powder
3 extra-large eggs
20 ml (¾ fl oz) neutral oil
80 ml (2 ½ fl oz) boiling water
1 ½ tsp lye water *or* ⅓ tsp baked bicarbonate of soda
   dissolved in 1 ½ tsp of water
rice flour, extra (for dusting)

1. Place the dry ingredients in a large bowl or the bowl of a food processor and mix to combine. A stand mixer fitted with a paddle attachment can also be used.

2. In a separate jug, whisk together the eggs and oil.

3. Pour the egg and oil mixture into the dry ingredients and mix on medium speed until it resembles breadcrumbs. Add the boiling water and lye water and continue mixing. A rough crumb will develop first, and then as it comes together, it will begin to roll around the bowl of the food processor, leaving the sides clean. Continue mixing until the dough is smooth. If mixing by hand, use a sturdy spoon or spatula to bring the dough together, then wet your hands and knead well for 8–9 minutes. The dough should be soft, warm and pliable; if it has not reached this point, continue to add boiling water by the teaspoon, mixing or processing consistently until it does.

4. Separate the dough into three equal portions and let rest in a ziplock bag for 5 minutes.

5. Working with one dough ball at a time, use a rolling pin to flatten it to about 0.5 cm (0.25 in) thick. Continue if rolling by hand, or begin feeding the dough through a pasta roller, dusting both sides of the dough with a little rice flour as necessary. You may need to feed it through a roller multiple times, folding and neatening on the widest setting to make the dough more workable. If necessary, lightly wet your fingers to add some moisture to the dough.

6. Roll the dough as thin as you would like your noodles, usually to the fourth or fifth setting on a roller, which is approximately 0.8–1 mm thick.

7. When the dough has been rolled into a thin sheet, generously dust it with rice flour and either feed it through a pasta cutter set to your desired width (the 'angel hair' or thinnest spaghetti setting is ideal for many Asian egg noodles dishes) or fold up the sheet to cut it by hand with a sharp knife.

8. Once cut, dust the noodles well with more rice flour and store in an airtight container until ready to use (the noodles also freeze very well at this stage).

9. To cook fresh or from frozen, bring a large saucepan of water to a rolling boil. Add the noodles and agitate with narrow tongs or chopsticks to separate them without breaking them up. The noodles cook very quickly (20–30 seconds if fresh, 40–50 seconds if frozen) so be vigilant or they will be soft and not perfectly chewy.

Lye Water and Baked Bicarbonate of Soda

Lye water is an alkaline solution that, when used sparingly, contributes to the bouncy chew or springiness of noodles and emphasizes yellow coloring. This is especially important in the making of gluten-free egg noodles due to the lack of gluten that is usually worked to help create that chewy texture.

Lye water can be difficult to find, but don't worry – you can easily make a homemade substitute by heating bicarbonate of soda in the oven, which transforms it into sodium carbonate, a stronger alkaline salt. It's a caustic substance that shouldn't come into contact with your bare skin (if it does, wash thoroughly with water) and shouldn't be directly inhaled, so work with some caution.

Lye water is an optional but *highly* recommended ingredient in my egg noodles. You can make a batch of the substitute that you can then keep on hand for other recipes or multiple portions of noodles. Simply follow these instructions (and always follow the specific recipe when using the baked bicarb):

1. Preheat your oven to 120°C (250°F). Line a large baking tray with aluminium foil. Sprinkle bicarbonate of soda in a thin layer over the foil (do as much as covers the whole pan or as little as you will use for a few noodle batches). Bake for 1 hour.

2. Once baked, remove the tray from the oven and set aside to cool completely.

3. When cooled, transfer the powder to an airtight container to use as needed.

Udon Noodles

Serves 3–4

My udon noodles are ideal to eat both in a simple broth (see page 67) or as thicker noodles to be stir-fried. The dough comes together very quickly and is highly workable, meaning it can also be rolled thinner or cut wider to suit varied applications. Although it uses a different blend of starches, this dough is the easiest to make and would be an ideal starting point for someone dipping their toe in the world of gluten-free noodle-making for the first time. As these noodles don't contain egg yolks, they can rely more heavily on the egg whites and the effect of boiling water on the starches to bind, meaning psyllium husk powder is not necessary.

60 g (2 oz) glutinous rice flour
40 g (1 ½ oz) rice flour
40 g (1 ½ oz) sweet potato starch
60 g (2 oz) tapioca starch
1 ½ tsp xanthan gum
1 tsp psyllium husk powder
2 extra-large egg whites
120 ml (4 fl oz) boiling water
rice flour, extra

1. Place the dry ingredients in a large bowl or the bowl of a food processor and mix to combine. A stand mixer fitted with a paddle attachment can also be used.

2. Add the egg whites, mix briefly, then add the boiling water and continue mixing. A rough crumb will develop first, and then as it comes together, it will begin to roll around the bowl of the food processor, leaving the sides clean. Continue mixing until the dough is smooth. If mixing by hand, use a sturdy spoon or spatula to bring the dough together, then knead well by hand for 8–9 minutes. The dough should be soft, warm and pliable.

3. Separate the dough into three equal portions and wrap two in plastic as you work on the third.

4. Lightly flour your work surface with rice flour and use the palms of your hands to flatten the dough into a thick disc. Switch to a rolling pin and roll out into a roughly rectangular sheet.

5. Roll the sheet initially to about 1 cm (½ in) thick, at which point you can either continue rolling by hand or switch to a mechanical pasta roller, dusting well with rice flour before doing so. If using a pasta roller, feed the sheet through the machine on the widest setting twice. If rolling by hand, roll out until the sheet is about 0.4 cm (⅛ in) thick.

6. Dust the sheet again with rice flour, then fold the dough up to cut. Fold the shorter edges inwards, as if rolling into a short, flat log. Use a sharp knife to cut through the folded layers of noodle dough, pausing to wipe down the knife as necessary.

7. With your fingers, separate the noodles and toss them to coat the cut edges with a little of the rice flour. Set aside until ready to cook, storing in an airtight container in the fridge if making them more than 30 minutes ahead of serving time.

8. To cook, bring a large pot of water to a rapid boil. Add the noodles and cook for 40–50 seconds until tender, agitating the noodles in the water with chopsticks or narrow tongs to separate them without breaking them up.

9. Drain the noodles and rinse them in hot water to remove any excess starch and to stop them from sticking together. Serve the noodles in a hot broth of your choice (see suggestion on page 67) or add them to a stir-fry.

Wonton Skins

Makes about 40

These wonton skins can be rolled extremely thin and have a very silky texture when boiled or steamed, making them perfect for wontons and siu mai. As is the case with the egg noodles, the higher proportion of egg yolks necessitates the inclusion of psyllium husk powder in the dough. These skins are very versatile as they can also be deep-fried to create a crispy, lightly puffed shell.

110 g (4 oz) Dumpling Flour Blend (page 11)
3¼ tsp psyllium husk powder
1 large egg plus 1 yolk
1 tsp neutral oil (vegetable or canola)
3 tbsp boiling water

1. Place the dry ingredients in a mixing bowl or the bowl of a food processor and mix to combine. A stand mixer fitted with a paddle attachment can also be used.

2. In a separate jug, whisk together the eggs and oil.

3. Pour the egg and oil mixture into the dry ingredients and mix on medium speed until it resembles breadcrumbs. Add the boiling water and continue mixing. A rough crumb will develop first, and then as it comes together, it will begin to roll around the bowl of the food processor, leaving the sides clean. Continue mixing until the dough is smooth. If mixing by hand, use a sturdy spoon or spatula to bring the dough together, then wet your hands and knead well for 8–9 minutes. The dough should be soft, warm and pliable.

4. Separate the dough into two portions and let rest in a ziplock bag for 5 minutes.

5. Working with one dough ball at a time, use a rolling pin to flatten it to about 5 mm (¼ in) thick. Continue if rolling by hand, or begin feeding the dough through a pasta roller, dusting both sides of the dough with a little rice flour as necessary. You may need to feed it through a roller multiple times, folding and neatening on the widest setting to make the dough more workable. If necessary, lightly wet your fingers to add some moisture to the dough.

6. Roll the dough out until it is slightly less than 1 mm thick (likely the sixth or seventh setting on a mechanical roller).

7. When the dough has been rolled into a thin sheet, dust it generously with rice flour and cut to the desired shape, either squares approximately 7 x 7 cm (2¾ x (2¾ in; cut with a sharp knife) or rounds approximately 8–9 cm (3¼–3½ in; cut with a cookie cutter) in diameter.

8. The wrappers can be stacked with a light dusting of rice flour between pieces and then stored in an airtight bag or container until use. If the wrappers are not being used within the hour, wrap the stack in paper towel and then place in the resting bag or container to refrigerate. Allow them to come to room temperature before you fold them.

Dumpling Wrappers

Makes 35–40   (DAIRY FREE) (EGG-FREE OPTION) (NUT FREE) (SOY FREE) (VEGETARIAN)

This dumpling wrapper recipe was the first I perfected after many years of trials and failures, so I'm very fond of it! It can be rolled very thin but is actually best when kept slightly thicker than wonton skins, approximately the same thickness as pasta. Although the dumplings made with this dough are delicious when boiled and steamed, they are the absolute best when pan-fried like Japanese gyōza, especially if paired with the crispy lattice base (see page 91).

These wrappers can be made egg-free, but more xanthan gum and some psyllium husk powder is needed. Add ½ tsp xanthan gum and 1 tsp of psyllium husk powder to the Dumpling Flour Blend and increase the quantity of boiling water to 130 ml (4 ½ fl oz). This dough will also work as an egg-free noodle option.

135 g (5 oz) Dumpling Flour Blend (page 11)
80 ml (2 ½ fl oz) boiling water
1 large egg white

1. Place the flour in a mixing bowl or the bowl of a food processor. A stand mixer fitted with a paddle attachment can also be used.

2. Add the egg white, mix briefly, then add the boiling water and continue mixing. A rough crumb will develop first, and then as it comes together, it will begin to roll around the bowl of the food processor, leaving the sides clean. Continue mixing until the dough is smooth. If mixing by hand, use a sturdy spoon or spatula to bring the dough together, then knead well by hand for 8–9 minutes. The dough should be soft, warm and pliable.

3. Separate the dough into two portions and let rest in a ziplock bag for 5 minutes.

4. Working with one dough ball at a time, use a rolling pin to flatten it to about 5 mm (¼ in) thick. Continue if rolling by hand, or begin feeding the dough through a pasta roller, dusting both sides of the dough with a little rice flour as necessary. You may need to feed it through a roller multiple times, folding and neatening on the widest setting to make the dough more workable. If necessary, lightly wet your fingers to add some moisture to the dough.

5. Roll the dough out until it is approximately 1.5 mm thick (which is usually about the fifth or sixth setting on a mechanical roller).

6. When the dough has been rolled into a thin sheet, dust it generously with rice flour and cut to the desired shape, either squares approximately 7 x 7 cm (2 ¾ x 2 ¾ in; cut with a sharp knife) or rounds approximately 8–9 cm (3 ¼–3 ½ in; cut with a cookie cutter) in diameter.

7. The wrappers can be stacked with a light dusting of rice flour between pieces and then stored in an airtight bag or container until use. If the wrappers are not being used within the hour, wrap the stack in paper towel and then place in the bag or container to refrigerate. Allow them to come to room temperature before you fold them.

Chow Mein

Serves 2–3

Noodle dishes like chow mein are among the most elusive in the gluten-free lifestyle. The noodles are bouncy, chewy and dry, in the best way! This was one of the first dishes I just *had* to make after I'd perfected my egg noodles. The trick is to steam the noodles rather than boil them, which keeps them from going soggy and allows them to actually crisp up a little when you stir-fry them afterwards. Because this is more of a dry-style noodle dish, as a bonus, it reheats really well, making it perfect for a midweek dinner when you can take leftovers to work the next day. I've kept this as a simple vegetarian dish, but you can absolutely customize it by adding protein like eggs, sliced meat or tofu.

2 spring onions (scallions)

150 g (5 ½ oz) bean sprouts

250 g (9 oz) thin Egg Noodles (page 58)

½ tbsp GF dark soy sauce

1 tbsp GF soy sauce

½ tbsp GF oyster sauce or vegetarian oyster sauce

1 ½ tsp caster (superfine) sugar

1 ½ tsp sesame oil

2–3 tbsp neutral oil

1 small brown onion, sliced

sesame seeds, to garnish

1. Prepare a large steamer over medium heat to pre-cook the noodles.

2. While the steamer heats, prepare the vegetables. Chop the spring onions into 6–7 cm (about 2 ½ in) pieces, separating the white parts from the green. Wash and drain the bean sprouts. Set aside.

3. Place the fresh, raw egg noodles into the steamer, spreading them out as much as possible. Steam covered for 4 minutes.

4. Once cooked, remove the noodles from the steamer and lay out over a clean kitchen surface. Spread the noodles out as much as possible, untangling any large clumps as you go.

5. While the noodles cool and dry, prepare the sauce by combining both the soy sauces, oyster sauce, caster sugar and sesame oil in a small bowl. Set aside.

6. When the noodles have cooled for 10–15 minutes, heat a wok or large frying pan over high heat. Add about a tablespoon of the oil and fry the brown onion for 20–30 seconds before adding the whites of the spring onions. Stir-fry for another 30–40 seconds, then tip into a bowl and set aside.

7. Add another tablespoon of oil to the hot wok or pan and add the noodles. Spread the noodles out as much as possible and leave to crisp up slightly for 20–30 seconds. Toss the noodles around and repeat, adding some extra oil as necessary.

8. Add the partially cooked onions, the spring onion greens and the bean sprouts and toss to combine. Then add the sauce mixture and toss well until it evenly coats all the noodles and vegetables.

9. Tip the chow mein into a serving dish and top with sesame seeds. Serve fresh and hot.

Shoyu Ramen

Serves 6

Making ramen from scratch can definitely seem a daunting task. It's a labour of love that makes for a bit of a project, but if you've been gluten-free for a while (and if you *live* for noodles, like me), I think you'll find this worth the effort. The cooking and preparation is spread over two days as the Ajitama and Chashu (see below) should be made beforehand. Whether this makes it more or less daunting is your call!

You could take a little shortcut by pairing my Egg Noodles (page 58, along with any of the toppings below) with the 5-minute Noodle Soup I often use for udon (see page 75). The flavor won't be as intense without the homemade meaty broth, but it will absolutely satisfy those noodle cravings.

Ajitama (or ramen eggs) (best made the day before)

- 6 eggs (at room temperature)
- 150 ml (5 fl oz) GF soy sauce
- 100 ml (3 ½ fl oz) GF mirin
- 50 ml (1 ¾ fl oz) sake
- 40 g (1 ½ oz) caster (superfine) sugar

Chashu pork (best made the day before)

- 1 kg (2 lb 3 oz) piece of boneless pork belly, skin off
- 2 garlic cloves
- 4 cm (1 ½ in) piece of ginger, sliced
- 2–3 dried shiitake mushrooms
- 90 g (3 oz) caster (superfine) sugar
- ½ tsp salt
- 100 ml (3 ½ fl oz) GF mirin
- 100 ml (3 ½ fl oz) sake
- 240 ml (8 fl oz) GF soy sauce

Broth

- 1 kg (2 lb 3 oz) pork bones
- 1 chicken frame
- 2 brown onions, peeled and halved
- 2 carrots, halved
- 500 ml (17 fl oz) boiling water
- 6–7 dried shiitake mushrooms
- 10 cm (4 in) piece of ginger
- 6 garlic cloves
- 2 pieces kombu (30–40 g or 1–1 ½ oz)
- 60 g (2 oz) katsuobushi (bonito flakes) or, if unavailable, 40 g (1 ½ oz) GF dashi stock powder

Assembly

- Egg Noodles (page 58)
- 2 spring onions (scallions)
- 1–2 tsp sesame oil
- dry-roasted seaweed, to serve (optional)

→

Ajitama (or ramen eggs)

1. Start by cooking and marinating the eggs (this is best done the day before serving the ramen but can also be done in the morning). Bring a large pot of water to the boil. Add eggs and cook for 6.5 minutes.

2. Meanwhile, combine the other ingredients in a sealable container or ziplock bag.

3. After 6.5 minutes, remove the eggs from the boiling water and submerge in cold water. Allow to cool.

4. Gently peel the eggs and submerge them in the soy sauce mixture. Seal the container and place in the fridge. Rotate the eggs in the sauce every few hours.

Chashu pork

1. Move on to the chashu, which is also best made in advance as the meat should cool completely in the fridge before slicing to serve. Start by rolling the pork belly into a tight log and trussing it with kitchen twine so that it will hold its shape.

2. Place the roll of pork belly in a pot large enough for the meat to be submerged and cover with cold water. Place over high heat and bring to a simmer before lowering the heat to medium-low. Simmer for 20 minutes.

3. Remove the pork and rinse under running water (do not unroll it), removing any scum stuck to the outside of the roll. Clean the pot, replace the pork and cover with fresh water (approximately 2 L or 68 fl oz).

4. Add the garlic, ginger and shiitake mushrooms and bring to a simmer. Add the caster sugar and salt, then place a drop lid onto the pork (you can use a lid slightly smaller than the pot – this will sit in the liquid on top of the pork to keep it submerged in the braising liquid). Simmer like this for 30 minutes.

5. Remove the drop lid and add the mirin, sake and soy sauce. Simmer uncovered for a further 75 minutes.

6. Turn off the heat but leave the pork sitting in the braising liquid for 10 minutes. Remove the pork and place it in a container or shallow bowl. Allow both the pork and the braising liquid to cool for about an hour before placing separately and covered in the fridge to cool completely.

Broth

1. Next, make the ramen broth (this should be started at least 5–6 hours before serving). Preheat oven to 200°C (390°F). In a large roasting tray, spread out the pork bones and chicken frame as much as possible to promote browning. Roast in the oven for 30 minutes.

2. Remove the tray from the oven and rotate the bones and chicken frame to brown on all sides. Add the onions and carrots to the roasting tray, then roast for another 30 minutes.

3. Remove the tray from the oven and transfer the bones and vegetables to a large stockpot. Pour 500 ml (17 fl oz) of boiling water into the roasting tray and scrape up any residue stuck on the bottom. Add this liquid to the stockpot with the bones.

4. Add 3–4 L (100–135 fl oz) of water (the bones should be nearly or totally submerged) and heat over medium-high heat. Add the remaining broth ingredients and bring the pot to a simmer.

5. When the kombu has softened and feels gummy (after 10–15 minutes of simmering), remove it and discard. Continue to gently simmer the rest of the stock for 3.5–4 hours, skimming regularly to remove any impurities or foam that rises to the surface. This is essential for a clear broth.

6. Turn off the heat and remove the larger chunks from the stock with tongs, a slotted spoon or kitchen spider. Add three-quarters of the reserved braising liquid from the chashu pork belly and taste. You may need to add more of the braising liquid to season the stock depending on how much water evaporated from both the stock and the braising liquid, so adjust according to taste.

7. Strain the soup well through a sieve lined with muslin or cheesecloth. You may need to strain twice to remove all impurities from the broth and be left with a richly colored but clear soup. Set the soup aside while you prepare other elements.

Assembly

1. Bring a large pot of water to the boil to cook the ramen noodles. Finely slice the spring onions and set aside. Remove the ajitama (ramen eggs) from the marinade and slice in half lengthways.

2. Cut thin slices off the chashu pork belly and lay them on an oven tray. Use a kitchen torch to scorch the slices, which reheats them and adds a smoky flavor.

3. Bring the ramen broth back to a simmer if necessary.

4. Cook the noodles according to directions on page 58. Once drained, drizzle the noodles with sesame oil and toss lightly to prevent them from clumping.

5. Serve immediately by placing a portion of noodles into a deep soup bowl. Submerge in a generous ladle of soup, then top with the ajitama (ramen egg), a couple of slices of pork belly and the spring onion. Garnish with the dry-roasted seaweed if desired.

Chicken and Ginger Udon Noodles

Serves 3–4

I live on stir-fries – making them is second nature, so I wasn't sure about including any stir-fry recipes in this book. But I've realized through my social media that a lot of gluten-free people struggle with quick, flavorful meals, and this is exactly that. You don't have to use my udon noodles (although I highly recommend it) – you can use whatever noodles you have on hand or simply serve this with rice. Either way, it's delicious, it comes together very quickly, and making dishes like this is a great way to get a feel for the balance of aromatics and sauces that you might not be familiar with. And once you get the hang of it, you'll be able to experiment with other meat and vegetable combinations to keep you going through a busy week.

1 chicken breast, sliced into 5–6 cm (2–2½ in) strips
2 tsp GF soy sauce
1 tsp GF oyster sauce
1 tsp caster (superfine) sugar
2 tsp sake
2 tsp GF cornstarch
3 tbsp neutral oil
2 portions of fresh Udon Noodles (see page 61)
3–4 garlic cloves, minced
2 cm (¾ in) piece of ginger, finely chopped
1 brown onion, peeled and sliced
7–8 baby corn spears, halved lengthwise
2 heads of bok choy, halved
½ red capsicum, sliced
1 tbsp GF soy sauce, extra
2 tbsp GF oyster sauce, extra
¼ tsp white pepper
2 tsp sesame oil
2 spring onions (scallions), finely sliced
200 ml (7 fl oz) GF chicken stock
2 tbsp water
1 tbsp GF cornstarch

1. Start by marinating the chicken strips. Place in a medium bowl and add the soy sauce, oyster sauce, caster sugar, sake and cornstarch. Mix well, cover and set aside for 30 minutes (place in the fridge if not cooking within 30 minutes).

2. Place a large pot of water over high heat for the noodles. While that comes to a boil, heat half of the oil in a large pan or wok over high heat.

3. Add the marinated chicken, spreading it around the pan as much as possible. Brown the meat on both sides but don't worry about cooking it all the way through. Remove from the pan and set aside.

4. Place the udon noodles into the pot of boiling water to cook while you finish the stir-fry (these will take 4–5 minutes to become tender).

5. Add the rest of the oil to the pan, then add the garlic and ginger and fry until fragrant. Add the vegetables and toss well. Add the extra soy and oyster sauces, white pepper and sesame oil. Toss to coat the vegetables well, then add the spring onions, reserving some of the green tops to garnish.

6. Return the chicken to the pan and toss to coat in the sauces. Add the chicken stock and place a lid on the pan to steam the vegetables.

7. Quickly make a cornstarch slurry by mixing the water into the cornstarch. Pour the slurry into the stir-fry and toss well. The sauce will thicken and become glossy.

8. Drain the cooked udon noodles and then add them to the stir-fry. Toss well to coat them in the sauce and to distribute them among the meat and vegetables.

9. Serve immediately, topping with some of the reserved spring onions.

BBQ Pork Belly with Egg Noodles

Serves 4–5

I never used to order dry egg noodle dishes, preferring to go for the saucy or soupy options that seemed more complicated and harder to make at home. Little did I realize how much effort goes into such a seemingly simple bowl of noodles! For this one, you'll need a portion of my Egg Noodles (page 58), and to marinate the pork for at least 8 hours, so be sure to get onto that beforehand. You'll be surprised how quickly this can come together once those are done (especially if you've got a handy stash of egg noodles in the freezer).

1 kg (2 lb 3 oz) pork belly, cut into strips
1 portion of Egg Noodles (page 58)
2–3 bok choy, steamed, to serve
1–2 tbsp neutral oil

Pork marinade

60 g (2 oz) sugar
1½ tsp salt
¼ tsp Chinese five spice
¼ tsp white pepper
1 tsp sesame oil
1½ tbsp GF Chinese cooking wine (Shaoxing variety, or Japanese cooking sake)
1½ tbsp GF soy sauce
1½ tbsp GF hoisin sauce
2 garlic cloves, minced
2 tbsp honey

Egg noodle seasoning

2 tsp sesame oil
1 tsp GF soy sauce
½ tsp caster (superfine) sugar
¼ tsp white pepper
¼ tsp GF chicken powder (optional)
½ tsp chilli oil (optional)

1. Combine the marinade ingredients in a large bowl and stir well. Set half aside in a small bowl, cover and refrigerate.

2. Add the pork belly strips to the large bowl and mix with your hands, ensuring all the pork is completely coated in the marinade. Cover and refrigerate for 8 hours or overnight.

3. When ready to cook, preheat your oven to 220°C (430°F). Place a roasting rack into a large baking tray and add just enough water to the tray to cover the base.

4. Arrange the pork belly strips on the rack so they don't touch, then roast the pork for 15 minutes.

5. Reduce the oven temperature to 190°C (375°F). Baste the pork with the reserved marinade, then return to the oven for another 25–30 minutes, turning and basting the pork twice more.

6. While the pork is cooking, prepare a large steamer over medium-high heat to pre-cook the noodles. Place the fresh, raw egg noodles into the steamer, spreading them out as much as possible. Place the lid on and steam for 5 minutes.

7. Once cooked, remove the noodles from the steamer and lay out over a clean kitchen surface, spreading them out as much as possible.

8. Allow the noodles to cool and dry for 10–15 minutes.

9. Prepare the egg noodle seasoning by combining all the ingredients in a medium bowl. Set aside.

10. When the pork is cooked, remove it from the oven, cover with aluminium foil and let it rest while you finish the noodles.

11. Heat a tablespoon of oil in a wok or large frying pan over high heat and add the cooled noodles. Spread them out as much as possible and leave to crisp up for 20–30 seconds. Toss and repeat, adding extra oil as necessary, then finish with the seasoning sauce. Toss well and remove from the heat.

12. Slice the pork belly into bite-size pieces. Portion out the noodles and top with the pork and steamed bok choy if desired.

5-minute Noodle Soup

Serves 1

Sometimes when a noodle craving hits, it's not to be denied! And making a ramen broth from scratch for a weeknight dinner is probably not something most of us want to do. This soup is the answer to my problem when I want a quick, comforting meal that's easy to bulk up with an egg or some vegetables. When I have homemade noodles in the freezer I will use those, but I also happily do this with dry rice noodles if that's all I have to hand. This soup also makes for easy clean-up, which is a bonus – if I'm adding any vegetables or an egg, I can cook those in the same pot that I'll cook the noodles in and then the soup can be made directly in your serving bowl. Just add boiling water! Given that we don't have many options for 'instant meals', this can be a lifesaver.

¾ tsp GF dashi stock powder

¾ tsp caster (superfine) sugar

a pinch of white pepper

1 tbsp GF soy sauce

1 tsp sake

½ tsp sesame oil

¼ tsp chill oil (optional)

1 portion GF noodles of choice

400 ml (13 ½ fl oz) boiling water

Optional toppings

spring onion (scallion), finely sliced

toasted seaweed, shredded

sesame seeds

1. Bring a large pot of water to the boil over high heat. While you're waiting, place all the ingredients except the noodles, boiling water and toppings in a large soup bowl.

2. When the water is boiling, add the noodles and cook according to the instructions. (If you're bulking up the meal with some vegetables or eggs, cook these in the water before the noodles.)

3. When the noodles are cooked, drain them, and rinse under hot running water to remove any excess starch and prevent them from sticking together.

4. Add the freshly boiled water to the ingredients in your soup bowl, stir briefly to dissolve the sugar and dashi powder, then add your noodles.

5. Top with any of the optional extras before serving.

Braised Beef with Noodles

Serves 4

Whenever I've got egg noodles ready in the freezer, this is one of my easy go-to meals. There's minimal effort involved because most of the flavor is developed through the braising process. If you've got a slow cooker or pressure cooker, this becomes even easier. Either way, it's a simple, comforting dish that will definitely hit the spot, especially if you've been gluten-free for a while, because this sort of GF food is so hard to find outside your own kitchen.

1 tbsp neutral oil

4 garlic cloves, peeled

5 cm (2 in) piece of ginger, sliced

500–700 g (about 1 lb 5 oz) chuck steak or other beef cut for stewing

60 ml (2 fl oz) GF soy sauce

2 tbsp GF oyster sauce

2½ tbsp sugar

2 tbsp GF Chinese cooking wine (Shaoxing variety, or Japanese cooking sake)

4 spring onions (scallions), white and green parts separated

500 ml (17 fl oz) water

4 portions of your favorite GF noodles

steamed bok choy or other greens, to serve

sesame seeds, to garnish

1. Heat the oil in a large saucepan over medium-low heat, then add the garlic and ginger and fry until fragrant.

2. Chop the beef into large (7–8 cm or 3 in) chunks and add them to the pan, searing on all sides.

3. Add the sauces, sugar, cooking wine, the whites of the spring onions and 500 ml (17 fl oz) of water. Bring it to a simmer, then place a lid on the saucepan and cook on medium-low heat for 90 minutes.

4. Remove the lid, raise the heat to medium and simmer uncovered for a further 60–75 minutes, or until the meat is fork-tender.

5. Keep warm while you prepare the noodles and steamed greens if desired. Slice the greens of the spring onion to garnish.

6. Portion out the cooked noodles, then top with steamed vegetables and a generous serving of the beef and braising liquid.

7. Top with spring onion and sesame seeds if desired and serve.

Chicken and Coriander Dumplings

Makes about 40

This section is my *favorite* part of the book. Anyone that knows me or has followed along with my cooking for a while will know that I'm obsessed with dumplings. The day I first made a dumpling wrapper dough that worked, I cried. I'm not kidding; I was so happy. These are just a few of the dumpling varieties I make regularly, so set aside time for some folding and let the gluten-free dumpling era reign!

2–3 chicken thigh fillets (300–350 g or about 12 oz)

2 tsp grated ginger

2 garlic cloves, minced

½ cup coriander (stem and leaves), finely chopped

1 spring onion (scallion), finely sliced

1 tbsp GF oyster sauce

2 tsp GF soy sauce

1 tbsp GF Chinese cooking wine (Shaoxing variety, or Japanese cooking sake)

2 tsp sesame oil

1 ½ tsp caster (superfine) sugar

½ tsp salt

2 tsp water

1 tbsp tapioca starch

1 portion of Dumpling Wrappers (cut into rounds) (page 63)

tapioca or rice flour, extra

1–2 tbsp neutral oil

1. Finely chop and then mince the chicken thigh fillets. You can substitute shop-bought mince or use a food processor, but chopping and mincing manually adds a succulent, meaty texture to the dumplings. Transfer to a mixing bowl.

2. Add the rest of the dumpling filling ingredients (except the extra flour and neutral oil) to the chicken and mix the dumpling filling very well with chopsticks or a wooden spoon.

3. Fold the dumplings using the triangular fold (see page 96) or your preferred folding method.

4. These dumplings are best pan-fried. Heat the neutral oil in a large frying pan over medium heat. Place the dumplings flat side down into the pan and allow them to brown – they should crisp as they cook.

5. Flip the dumplings over, then add 3–4 tbsp of water to the pan to ensure the seams of the dumplings cook through as well.

6. Serve the dumplings hot with a dipping sauce of your choice.

Pork and Prawn Wontons with Chilli Oil

Makes about 40

If you like spicy, aromatic, slippery wontons, then look no further! These are really simple to make and cook because the folding technique isn't as important as for some of the other dumplings. Because these get boiled, the important thing is to seal in the filling, but beyond that, you can really close them as haphazardly as you like. Boiling them also means that they're quite low maintenance – just cook them in a pot of boiling water for a few minutes and they're ready to go. I like to eat these with my Chilli Oil but they're also delicious when drizzled with my Simple Dipping Sauce (page 93) if spiciness isn't your thing.

300 g (10 ½ oz) pork mince

3 garlic cloves, minced

2 ½ tsp grated ginger

2 spring onions (scallions), finely sliced

¼ tsp white pepper

½ tsp GF chicken powder (optional)

½ tsp salt (if not using chicken powder, add an extra ¼ tsp)

1 tsp caster (superfine) sugar

1 tsp GF soy sauce

1 tsp GF Chinese cooking wine (use cooking sake if Shaoxing or similar is unavailable)

2 tsp sesame oil

2 tsp GF oyster sauce

2 tsp water

1 tbsp tapioca or rice flour, plus extra for folding

150 g (5 ½ oz) raw prawns (shrimp), peeled and deveined

1 portion of Wonton Skins, cut into squares (page 62)

Chilli Oil, to serve (page 93)

spring onion (scallion), to serve

1. Place the mince in a large bowl with all of the filling ingredients except for the prawns.

2. Roughly dice 100 g (3 ½ oz) of the prawns and add them to the bowl, then use a food processor to blitz the remaining 50 g (1 ¾ oz) into a rough paste. This will add prawn flavor to the mince while the chunks add a meaty texture.

3. Mix the dumpling filling well with chopsticks or a wooden spoon until almost a paste-like consistency as opposed to a chunky meatball consistency. This will happen as the protein in the meat breaks down with stirring.

4. Fold the dumplings using the alternative wonton fold (see page 97) or your preferred method.

5. To cook, bring a large pot of water to the boil. Season lightly with salt, then add the wontons. Boil for 3–5 minutes before testing for doneness.

6. Serve hot with Chilli Oil (page 93) and finely sliced spring onion.

Vegetarian Dumplings

Makes about 40

Gluten-free and vegetarian? No problem! This filling might not have meat but it's *packed* with flavor. I make these regularly because I generally have tofu in the fridge, which means I can satisfy my dumpling cravings without a trip to the shops.

2 dried shiitake mushrooms
1 tbsp neutral oil
1 tsp grated ginger
2 garlic cloves, finely chopped
1 medium carrot, peeled and finely grated
60 g (2 oz) Chinese cabbage, finely shredded
4–5 button mushrooms, finely chopped
1 spring onion (scallion), finely sliced
250 g (9 oz) firm tofu
1 tbsp GF oyster sauce or vegetarian oyster sauce
1 tsp GF soy sauce
1 tsp GF sake
1 tsp sesame oil
1 tsp caster (superfine) sugar
½ tsp salt
¼ tsp white pepper
1 tbsp tapioca starch
1 portion of Dumpling Wrappers (cut into rounds) (page 63)
tapioca or rice flour, extra
1–2 tbsp neutral oil, extra

1. Soak the shiitake mushrooms in a bowl of boiling water for 15–20 minutes.

2. Heat the oil in a large frying pan. Add the ginger and garlic and cook until fragrant. Add the carrot, cabbage and mushrooms and fry over medium heat until fully cooked through. Toss the spring onion through the other vegetables, then set aside to cool slightly.

3. Break up the tofu block into a mixing bowl, crumbling it between your fingers until it resembles mince. Add the cooked vegetables and stir to combine.

4. Add the rest of the dumpling filling ingredients (except the extra flour and oil) and stir well to distribute the seasonings through the tofu and vegetables.

5. Squeeze excess water out of the shiitake mushrooms, then finely dice and mix them into the filling.

6. Fold the dumplings using the ingot fold (see page 98) or your preferred folding method.

7. These dumplings are best steamed or pan-fried. To steam, prepare a steamer by lining the base with a piece of baking paper (cut or pierce some small holes in the paper to allow steam to pass through). Greasing the paper with a little sesame oil will add flavor and allow the dumplings to be more easily removed after cooking. Steam the dumplings for 8–10 minutes on medium-high heat before testing for doneness.

8. To pan-fry, heat the neutral oil in a large frying pan over medium heat. Place the dumplings flat side down into the pan and allow them to brown – they should crisp as they cook. Flip the dumplings over, then add 3–4 tbsp of water to the pan to ensure the seams of the dumplings cook through as well.

9. Serve the dumplings hot with a dipping sauce of your choice.

Steamed Prawn Dumplings

Makes about 40

DAIRY FREE **NUT FREE**

These are inspired by har gow, a Cantonese shrimp dumpling that you might have come across before as a gluten-free option. They're usually made with wheat starch in combination with other starches, and some restaurants have realized that the wheat starch can be omitted without compromising on the deliberately sticky, chewy texture of the wrapping. While har gow are delicious, I prefer to use my dumpling wrappers because they're thinner and easier to work with, meaning you can stuff even more prawns inside them! I've also opted for a slightly more aromatic filling because I think it complements the prawns really well.

400 g (14 oz) raw prawns (shrimp), peeled and deveined

2 garlic cloves, minced

1 ½ tsp grated ginger

1 spring onion (scallion), finely sliced

¼ tsp white pepper

½ tsp GF chicken powder (optional)

¼ tsp salt (if not using chicken powder, add an extra ¼ tsp)

½ tsp caster (superfine) sugar

1 tsp GF soy sauce

1 tsp GF Chinese cooking wine (use cooking sake if Shaoxing or similar is unavailable)

1 tsp sesame oil

1 tbsp tapioca or rice flour, plus extra for folding

1 portion of Dumpling Wrappers, cut into rounds (page 63)

1. Roughly dice 300 g (10 ½ oz) of the prawns and add them to a mixing bowl, then use a food processor to blitz the remaining 100 g (3 ½ oz) into a rough paste. Combine with the chopped prawns.

2. Add the rest of the ingredients for the filling and mix well with chopsticks or a wooden spoon.

3. Seal the dumplings using your preferred folding method (see pages 96–101) or feel free to experiment with something more intricate. As steaming is a gentle cooking method, there's a little more room for error.

4. Prepare a steamer by lining the base with a piece of baking paper (cut or pierce some small holes in the paper to allow steam to pass through). Greasing the paper with a little sesame oil will add flavor and allow the dumplings to be more easily removed after cooking. Steam the dumplings for 8–10 minutes on medium-high heat before testing for doneness.

5. Serve hot with a dipping sauce of your choice.

Fried Wontons

Makes about 40

DAIRY FREE · NUT FREE

I don't make these very often, simply because deep-frying regularly is obviously not ideal, but when I do, I make plenty of them because they're so delicious! They're meaty, crunchy and completely moreish. Be sure to serve them piping hot because the meat juice will soften the crispy shell after a while.

---

100 g (3 ½ oz) Chinese cabbage, finely chopped

½ tsp salt

300 g (10 ½ oz) pork mince

3 garlic cloves, minced

1 spring onion (scallion), finely sliced

100 g (3 ½ oz) canned water chestnuts, drained and finely chopped

1 tbsp GF soy sauce

1 tbsp GF Chinese cooking wine (Shaoxing variety, or Japanese cooking sake)

1 tsp sesame oil

1 tsp caster (superfine) sugar

½ tsp salt, extra

¼ tsp white pepper

2 tsp tapioca starch

1 portion of Wonton Skins, cut into squares (page 62)

tapioca or rice flour, extra

neutral oil, for frying

1. Place the cabbage in a medium bowl and sprinkle the salt over it. Massage the salt in with your fingers, then set the bowl aside for 10 minutes.

2. Meanwhile, combine the pork mince, garlic and spring onion. Add the water chestnuts to the mixture along with the rest of the dumpling filling ingredients (except the extra starch and neutral oil).

3. Squeeze as much liquid out of the cabbage as possible, then add that to the dumpling filling. Mix well with chopsticks or a wooden spoon until it has an almost paste-like consistency as opposed to a chunky meatball consistency.

4. Fold the dumplings using the fried wonton fold (see page 99) or your preferred folding method.

5. To cook the wontons, heat about 10 cm (4 in) of oil in a saucepan for deep-frying over medium-high heat. The oil is ready when a wooden spoon or chopstick sizzles when the end is dipped in. Fry the wontons until they are crisp and golden brown, then allow them to drain slightly on a cooling rack or sheet of paper towel.

6. Serve fresh and hot with your desired dipping sauce.

Prawn and Chicken Siu Mai

Makes about 40

Siu mai, also known as shumai, are an open-topped dumpling variety. Rather than pleating the wrappers to seal closed completely, with these, the wrapper forms almost a bucket shape around a plump pile of the filling. This technique is tricky to master (I still need a lot of practice) while still being quite a quick option for those new to dumpling folds. And because they're steamed and not pan-fried, they're a little more forgiving of imperfection.

3 dried shiitake mushrooms

200 g (7 oz) raw prawns (shrimp), peeled and deveined

350 g (12 ½ oz) chicken mince

3 garlic cloves, minced

2 tsp grated ginger

1 spring onion (scallion), finely sliced

¼ tsp white pepper

½ tsp GF chicken powder (optional)

½ tsp salt (if not using chicken powder, add an extra ¼ tsp)

1 tsp caster (superfine) sugar

2 tsp GF soy sauce

1 ½ tsp GF Chinese cooking wine (use cooking sake if Shaoxing or similar is unavailable)

2 tsp sesame oil

1 tbsp GF oyster sauce

1 tbsp water

1 tbsp tapioca or rice flour, plus extra for folding

1 portion of Wonton Skins, cut into squares (page 62)

fish roe or small carrot, for garnish

2–3 tbsp frozen peas, for garnish

1. Soak the shiitake mushrooms in a bowl of boiling water for 15–20 minutes.

2. Roughly dice the prawns and add them to a mixing bowl with the chicken mince.

3. Add the rest of the ingredients for the filling and mix well with chopsticks or a wooden spoon until almost a paste-like consistency as opposed to a chunky meatball consistency. This will happen as the protein in the meat breaks down with stirring.

4. Squeeze excess water out of the mushrooms, then finely dice and mix them into the filling.

5. Fold the dumplings using the siu mai fold (see page 100) or your preferred folding method.

6. If using carrot to garnish the siu mai, peel and dice the carrot very finely, then place a small scoop of the carrot on top of the filling in each one. Top with a single frozen pea. If garnishing with roe, only add the pea and wait until after steaming to top with a small scoop of the roe.

7. To cook the siu mai, prepare a steamer by lining the base with a piece of baking paper (cut or pierce some small holes in the paper to allow steam to pass through). Greasing the paper with a little sesame oil will also add flavor and allow the dumplings to be more easily removed after cooking. Steam the dumplings for 8–10 minutes on medium-high heat before testing for doneness.

8. Serve hot with a dipping sauce of your choice.

Pan-fried Pork and Ginger Dumplings

Makes about 40

These dumplings resemble Japanese gyōza, also known as potstickers (although my filling does differ a little). I'd say these are most easily recognized thanks to the crispy lattice or 'skirt' that often accompanies them. This is achieved by pouring a starch, oil and water solution over the dumplings while they cook. The water evaporates, creating steam that cooks the top of the dumplings, and the oil cooks the starch in the pan, crisping up to become a crunchy base layer. Done perfectly, this can be turned out in one piece, as the dumplings get stuck together by the starch, but it can be tricky to nail the technique. Rest assured, though, that even if your lattice isn't perfect, the extra starch in the pan will still give the base of your dumplings the most delectable texture you can imagine!

500 g (1 lb 2 oz) pork mince

3 garlic cloves, minced

1 tbsp grated ginger

2 spring onions (scallions), finely sliced

¼ tsp white pepper

½ tsp GF chicken powder (optional)

¼ tsp salt (if not using chicken powder, add an extra ¼ tsp)

1 tsp caster (superfine) sugar

2½ tsp GF soy sauce

1 tsp sake

1 tsp sesame oil

2 tsp GF oyster sauce

1 egg

2 tsp tapioca starch

1 portion of Dumpling Wrappers, cut into rounds (page 63)

tapioca or rice flour, extra (for folding)

1 tbsp neutral oil

Crispy lattice (optional)

1½ tbsp rice flour

2 tbsp neutral oil

4 tbsp water

⅛ tsp salt

½ tsp sesame oil

1. Combine all the filling ingredients in a large bowl and mix well with chopsticks or a wooden spoon until almost a paste-like consistency as opposed to a chunky meatball consistency.

2. Fold the dumplings using the pleated half-moon fold (see page 101) or your preferred folding method.

3. If not cooking with a lattice, lightly oil a large, non-stick frying pan and place on a medium-high heat. Arrange the dumplings in the pan and allow them to brown for 4–5 minutes. Add 3–4 tbsp of water to the pan and cover with a lid so that the tops of the dumplings steam for another 4–5 minutes. The dumplings are ready when their seams have changed color and softened.

4. If cooking with the crispy lattice, place all lattice ingredients except the sesame oil in a small jug or bowl and whisk well to combine.

5. Lightly oil a large, non-stick frying pan and place on a medium-high heat. Arrange the dumplings in the pan, leaving about ½ cm (¼ in) between each one. Allow them to cook uncovered for 2–3 minutes.

6. When the bottom of the dumplings are just starting to crisp and brown, pour the lattice mixture all over the pan. Work quickly and try to cover as much of the surface area of the pan as possible. It should bubble, spit and start cooking straight away, so cover with a lid and leave it for 4–5 minutes.

→

7. When the dumpling skins look cooked (they should have changed color and softened), remove the lid. Sprinkle the sesame oil over the dumplings, and continue to cook until the water has evaporated from the lattice, leaving only the crisped starch (about 6–8 minutes). There will be some excess oil in the pan but this can be drained or wiped away later. If the tops of the dumplings seem to be drying out while the lattice cooks, brush them with a little water, but not enough to drip onto the lattice. You can also check to make sure the dumplings aren't burning by gently lifting a dumpling from the edge, but be careful as the attached lattice will snap if crisp and bent too far.

8. When the lattice is crisp and any excess water or starch has cooked or evaporated, remove the pan from the heat. Hold the dumplings in place with a large spatula and gently tilt the pan to discard any excess oil.

9. Agitate the pan a little to make sure the dumplings aren't sticking (the dumplings and lattice should be able to slide around in one piece). Place a large plate serving side down on top of the dumplings (it is best if the plate fits just inside the frying pan). Holding the plate in or on the pan with one hand and the handle of the frying pan in the other, quickly flip the pan so that the plate is on the bottom. Lift the pan away, revealing the dumplings arranged crisp side up on the plate.

10. Serve hot with a dipping sauce of your choice.

Chilli Oil

DAIRY FREE   EGG FREE   NUT FREE   SOY FREE   VEGAN

Chilli oil is a staple in my fridge and although you can usually find gluten-free versions reasonably easily, it's even easier to make at home. This is the simplest version I make and I love it like this, but feel free to customize it with your favorite spices if that's what you like. I store mine in a clean jar in the fridge where it can keep for several months (although it never lasts that long because I use it nearly every day).

100 ml (3 ½ fl oz) neutral oil
1 ½ tbsp chilli flakes
1 ½ tbsp chilli powder
½ tbsp caster (superfine) sugar
1 ¾ tsp salt
2 garlic cloves, minced

1. Heat oil in a small saucepan over medium heat.
2. Place other ingredients in a heatproof bowl.
3. When the oil is hot (shimmering but not smoking – the end of a wooden chopstick or spoon should sizzle if dipped in the oil), remove from the heat and pour over the ingredients in the bowl.
4. When the sizzling has subsided, stir to combine, then set aside until cool.
5. Store in a clean jar in the fridge.

Simple Dipping Sauce

DAIRY FREE   EGG FREE   NUT FREE   VEGAN

This is my go-to dumpling dipping sauce. It's salty and a little sweet, with a tang from the vinegar that goes perfectly with rich, juicy dumplings. I make this as I need it while I'm waiting for my dumplings to cook, but you could make it in advance and store in the fridge for up to a week.

2 tbsp GF soy sauce
2 tbsp GF mirin
1 ½ tbsp white or black rice vinegar
1 tsp sesame oil
1–2 tsp Chilli Oil (above, optional)

1. Place all ingredients except the Chilli Oil in a small bowl and mix to combine.
2. Add Chilli Oil to taste.
3. Serve with steamed, boiled or pan-fried dumplings.

Everything Sauce

I call this an Everything Sauce because it can be served with, well, just about everything. It's delicious on dumplings, steamed Asian greens, a simple block of silken tofu, eggs, rice etc. It really is very versatile. There's some more preparation required for this sauce than for the others, but it is definitely worth it! You can also prepare it in advance and store it in a jar in the fridge for up to a week or so.

2–3 cm (1 in) piece of ginger, peeled
3 garlic cloves, peeled
2 long red chillies (optional)
1 spring onion (scallion), roughly chopped
1 bunch coriander (leaves and stems)
1 tbsp sugar
1 tsp black sesame seeds
½ tsp salt
60 ml (2 fl oz) neutral oil
¼ tsp white pepper
2 tbsp white rice vinegar
2 ½ tbsp GF soy sauce
1 ½ tsp GF mirin
1 ½ tsp sesame oil

1. Place the shallot, ginger, garlic, chillies (remove the seeds to lessen the spice level) and the white part of the spring onion into a food processor. Remove and set aside the leaves from the coriander, then add the stems to the processor (discard the root).

2. Pulse until all the ingredients are finely chopped without being minced, stirring as necessary between pulses.

3. Place the finely chopped ingredients into a medium heatproof bowl.

4. Add the sugar, black sesame seeds and salt.

5. Heat the oil in a small saucepan over medium heat. When the oil is hot (shimmering but not smoking – the end of a wooden chopstick or spoon should sizzle if dipped in the oil), remove from the heat and pour over the ingredients in the bowl.

6. When the sizzling has subsided, stir to combine.

7. Add the white pepper, white rice vinegar, soy sauce, mirin and sesame oil.

8. Finely slice the coriander leaves and green portion of the spring onion, and add to the sauce.

9. Serve with steamed rice, vegetables, tofu, noodles, dumplings, eggs or grilled meats.

Dumpling Folding Methods

Triangular fold

1. Prepare a workstation with the bowl of your desired filling, a stack of round wrappers (keep the main stack covered with plastic to stop them drying out as you work), a small bowl of water and a small bowl containing the extra tapioca or rice flour.

2. Place about a teaspoon of dumpling filling in the centre of the wrapper. Wet your finger with water to moisten the outer edges of the wrapper and then use your forefingers and thumbs to bring the edges together in three sections, meeting in the middle. By pinching the middle together and then applying pressure along the seams of the three sections, you'll create a triangular dumpling that can sit flat with the seams facing upwards. If at any point there is too much moisture in the wrapper, causing the dough to become soggy or slide rather than stick as you bring the edges together, dip your finger in the tapioca or rice flour and apply it to the wet spot on the wrapper.

3. Once folded, place the dumpling on a lightly floured plate or tray.

4. Continue until you run out of wrappers or filling (note that any excess can be frozen). If the dumplings are touching on the plate or tray as you work, dust the tops lightly with tapioca or rice flour to prevent them from sticking to each other as the dough may rip when they are pulled apart.

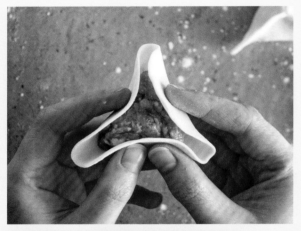

Wonton Fold

1. Prepare a workstation with the bowl of your desired filling, a stack of wrappers (keep the main stack covered with plastic to stop them drying out as you work), a small bowl of water and a small bowl containing the extra tapioca or rice flour.

2. Holding a wrapper with a corner pointing towards you in a diamond shape, place about a teaspoon of the filling in the centre. Wet your finger with water to moisten the top half of the wrapper around and above the filling.

3. Fold the wrapper corner closest to you up and over the filling, lining that corner up with the highest point of the diamond, and apply gentle pressure to seal it all the way around the filling.

4. It should now look like a triangle pointing away from you, with a point to the right and left of the sealed filling. Wet one of these corners with a little bit of water then bring in the other side corner to overlap with it, gently pressing them together. If at any point there is too much moisture in the wrapper, causing the dough to become soggy or slide rather than stick as you fold, dip your finger in the tapioca or rice flour and apply it to the wet spot on the wrapper.

5. Once folded, place the wonton on a lightly floured plate or tray. Continue until you run out of wrappers or filling (note that any excess can be frozen). If the wontons are touching on the plate or tray as you work, dust the tops lightly with tapioca or rice flour to prevent them from sticking to each other as the dough may rip when they are pulled apart.

Ingot fold

1. Prepare a workstation with the bowl of your desired filling, a stack of round wrappers (keep the main stack covered with plastic to stop them drying out as you work), a small bowl of water and a small bowl containing the extra tapioca or rice flour.

2. Place about a teaspoon of dumpling filling in the centre of the wrapper. Wet your finger with water to moisten the outer edges of the wrapper and then fold one edge over the filling, aligning it with the other side. Seal well without pleating so you have a semicircular dumpling with a flat, even seal.

3. Moisten one of the corners, then bring the two points together until they overlap, pressing the dry corner onto the moistened one. The flat outer seal will fold up against the pocket of filling as you do this to create a small round dumpling with a fold of wrapping around the outside. Note that if at any point there is too much moisture in the wrapper, causing the dough to become soggy or slide rather than stick as you fold, dip your finger in the tapioca or rice flour and apply it to the wet spot on the wrapper.

4. Once folded, place the dumpling on a lightly floured plate or tray. Continue until you run out of wrappers or filling (note that any excess can be frozen). If the dumplings are touching on the plate or tray as you work, dust the tops lightly with tapioca or rice flour to prevent them from sticking to each other as the dough may rip when they are pulled apart.

Fried Wonton Fold

1. Prepare a workstation with the bowl of your desired filling, a stack of square wrappers (keep the main stack covered with plastic to stop them drying out as you work), a small bowl of water and a small bowl containing a little extra tapioca or rice flour.

2. Holding the wrapper with a corner pointing towards you in a diamond shape, place about a teaspoon of dumpling filling in the centre of the wonton wrapper. Wet your finger with water to moisten the top half of the wrapper around and above the filling.

3. Fold the wrapper corner closest to you up and over the filling, lining that corner up with the highest point of the diamond, but do not press down yet. Bring the edges together, pleating and pressing as you go to create a flared effect above the bulge of the filling.

4. Be sure to seal it well to prevent it from breaking open while frying. If at any point there is too much moisture in the wrapper, causing the dough to become soggy or slide rather than stick as you fold, dip your finger in the tapioca or rice flour and apply it to the wet spot on the wrapper.

5. Once folded, place the wontons on a lightly floured plate or tray. Continue until you run out of wrappers or filling (note that any excess can be frozen). If the wontons are touching on the plate or tray as you work, dust the tops lightly with tapioca or rice flour to prevent them from sticking to each other as the dough may rip when they are pulled apart.

Siu Mai Fold

1. Prepare a workstation with the bowl of your desired filling, a stack of the square Wonton Skins (keep the main stack covered with plastic to stop them drying out as you work), a small bowl of water and a small bowl containing the extra tapioca or rice flour.

2. Form an 'O' shape with your thumb and forefinger, and place one of the wrappers over it.

3. Place a large tablespoon of filling in the centre of the wrapper, pressing it gently so that it moulds into the 'O' shape you created. Continue to press the filling down into that shape so the edges of the wrapper gather around the filling. Moisten the wrapper as necessary to stick any excess folds of wrapping neatly to the outside of the siu mai. Apply pressure around the outside of the dumpling to compress it into a uniform bucket-like shape.

4. Once finished, place the dumpling on a lightly floured plate or tray. Continue until you run out of wrappers or filling (note that any excess can be frozen).

Pleated Half-moon Fold

1. Prepare a workstation with the bowl of your desired filling, a stack of wrappers (keep the main stack covered with plastic to stop them drying out as you work), a small bowl of water and a small bowl containing the extra tapioca or rice flour.

2. Place about a teaspoon of dumpling filling in the centre of a wrapper. Wet your finger with water to moisten the outer edges of the wrapper and then fold one edge over the filling, pleating it into the other edge and sealing the filling inside. If at any point there is too much moisture in the wrapper, causing the dough to become soggy or slide rather than stick as you fold, dip your finger in the tapioca or rice flour and apply it to the wet spot on the wrapper.

3. Once folded, place the dumpling on a lightly floured plate or tray. Continue until you run out of wrappers or filling (note that any excess can be frozen). If the dumplings are touching on the plate or tray as you work, dust the tops lightly with tapioca or rice flour to prevent them from sticking to each other as the dough may rip when they are pulled apart.

Breads, Buns and Doughnuts

Baking bread is an art form, plain and simple.
There are always a lot of variables involved, and this is possibly even more true for gluten-free baking simply due to the longer list of ingredients required. The recipes I have created produce delicious bread and bread products, but they can be subject to those variables like any other, so before you tackle them, read through this introduction to get a feel for some of the key things to watch out for. The recipes themselves are also quite detailed to give as much information as possible and allow you to bake all the goodies in this chapter perfectly. However, if things don't go quite according to plan on the first attempt, try not to be discouraged – sometimes things happen that are simply out of your control, especially if subtle changes in temperature or humidity affect the results. Be patient, though, because you *can* and *will* get the hang of bread with some practice!

Warm Water

The first thing to note in the making of my bread recipes is the use of warm water as an ingredient. Ideally, this is water at the optimum temperature to activate the instant dried yeast, which is around 38–40°C (100–105°F). You can use a thermometer to check this accurately, or simply test it with your finger. It should be about the right temperature for a bath.

It should also be noted that I always weigh the water in my bread recipes for accuracy. I would recommend doing the same because, even though 1 g of water equates to 1 ml, I find that the levels on beakers are quite commonly incorrectly marked.

Yeast

I use an active dried yeast for all my bread recipes. I find it's the easiest to keep alive and on hand. You can use fresh yeast if that is what you're used to working with though. It's important to store your yeast properly as otherwise it won't function to help the bread rise, which is especially needed in gluten-free baking because of the heaviness of the dough. I store my yeast in the freezer sealed with an additional layer of plastic under the cap of the tin. Almost all my recipes start by blooming the yeast in the warm water with some sugar, which conveniently will indicate whether your yeast is okay to use. Once 'bloomed' after 5–10 minutes in a warm, draft-free spot, you should see a thick layer of foam on top of the water. If there is no foam, it's likely that your yeast is no longer viable. Get new yeast and try again.

Psyllium Husk and Xanthan Gum

You will always find psyllium husk and xanthan gum in my bread recipes as they're an essential ingredient in the making of a pliable dough. For more information about these ingredients, see the Pantry Staples list (page 5).

Baking Powder

Baking powder is not commonly used in regular bread baking. However, I find that due to the density of the gluten-free bread dough and its tendency to be heavy, it can benefit from the use of other leavening agents in addition to the yeast.

Sugar

Some bakers might be surprised at the amount of sugar present in many of the baked goods I've included in the book. As much as it is there for a sweet flavor, the sugar also operates as an essential food source for the yeast. Sugar is almost always added in two batches: initially with the water and yeast, providing food for the yeast to bloom, then again in the main dough with the other dry ingredients. This provides more food for the yeast to consume during the first bulk ferment and the second prove, and contributes significantly to the light, fluffy end result.

Bulk Fermentation

Most of my bread-based recipes will go through two proving processes. The first involves the dough resting in a single quantity. After mixing or kneading, the dough is transferred to a lightly greased bowl and covered with plastic wrap and then a dish towel (this helps to keep a moist, humid environment). This step, as well as the final prove, should be carried out in a warm, draft-free environment. There are a few ways to best ensure that the dough is resting in the right conditions. If your cooking space or another room in your house is generally naturally warm or can be heated, leaving the bowl on a counter should be adequate. You can also manufacture a warm space in a few different ways:

- Place the bowl in the oven (turned off) with a tray of freshly boiled water in the bottom. This can be problematic, however, as you often need to preheat the oven prior to the dough finishing its final prove.
- You can also heat a cup of water in the microwave for 1–2 minutes, turn it off, place the sealed bowl inside, then close the door, leaving the hot water inside.
- If you have an electric laundry dryer, run it (empty) for 4–5 minutes, then turn it off and place the bowl inside with the door closed. This will be adequate for the bulk ferment but probably won't work for the final prove as oven trays are unlikely to fit inside.
- Placing the bowl on top of the fridge, if possible, can also be a naturally warm location.

Shaping

After the bulk ferment, the bread dough is kneaded to make it smooth and ready to shape. Shaping gluten-free dough can be slightly more difficult than shaping 'normal' dough as it is never going to be as flexible or pliable. There is also a very fine line to walk between incorporating too much extra starch or moisture at this stage. Be sure to follow the instructions in the recipe closely as I've made them as detailed as possible.

Larger loaves and baguettes are quite simple to shape, but they are not 'laminated' in the way a 'normal' loaf is. This is because gluten-free breads require a different level of hydration, which also makes them less malleable.

The most difficult doughs to shape are the sweet buns that are twisted or braided in some way. Handle the dough very gently and don't lift the buns high off the work surface as you work with them because the weight of any hanging dough will likely cause it to stretch beyond breaking point.

Second Prove

The second prove happens following the bulk ferment, after the dough has been kneaded and shaped. This gives the yeast an opportunity to lift the dough while it is in the shape that will be baked. For the final prove, the rolls, buns or loaves should be returned to the warm, draft-free area and covered loosely with plastic (so as to not inhibit the rise) and then a dish towel. This second prove is usually 45 minutes to an hour. If left longer, the dough will be at risk of over-proving, which can cause the baked goods to collapse in the oven.

→

Scoring

Some of the recipes in this book require the proved dough to be scored. Scoring is a way to control the rise of the bread when it goes in the oven and is responsible for the aesthetic patterns and 'ears' (where one side of the scored dough curls away from the body of the loaf as it rises) seen on professionally baked loaves. Scoring creates a weak spot in the loaf through which the bread can rise during cooking. Without scoring, the natural weak spots in the loaf will break instead, causing it to rise haphazardly.

To score a loaf, you'll need a small, sharp knife or bread lame, a baking tool with a razor blade attached to a handle for ease of use. For a gluten-free loaf, I find that scoring a little deeper (1–1.5 cm or about ½ in) than what is conventional helps shape the loaf in the oven. While the design imparted by the scoring is largely aesthetic, the angle of the scoring is important. Scoring should be done by a knife or lame positioned at a 45-degree angle from the surface of the bread to optimize the rise and the release of steam during cooking without creating a flap that is too heavy to be lifted by the steam. This is simple enough when scoring directly into the top of the loaf but should also be kept in mind when scoring on the sides or outer edges, as this may be slightly counter-intuitive. See the diagram below for an illustration of the ideal scoring angle based on the location of the cut.

Cooking

You will notice that the cooking times and methods for the bread recipes in this book vary quite drastically. This is dependent on the individual variations in ingredients and resultant hydration in each product, as well as the shape and size of the bread that is being cooked. Smaller buns with thinner layers of dough can require as little as 14–16 minutes and don't require any special attention in terms of added steam or temperature control. Larger loaves differ, usually needing 1–2 hours of baking time and the addition of ice or cold water in a hot tray in the base of the oven during cooking. This creates steam when the loaf is introduced to the hot oven, which helps with what is known as 'oven lift', the immediate, large rise that happens in the early stage of baking that requires steam as well as high heat. The larger loaves also require a temperature change, as the first part of cooking browns the bread and promotes rising at high heat, while the second part of baking cooks the loaf through, reducing the internal moisture of the loaf at a lower heat. Be patient and always follow the written recipe as closely as possible because undercooking the bread will result in a dense, gummy, possibly collapsed loaf, while overcooking will create a dry loaf with an overly thick or burnt crust. Where possible, especially if you're not very familiar with your oven, use an oven thermometer to ensure accuracy in cooking time and temperature.

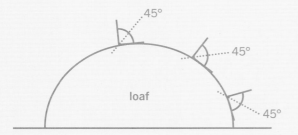

Storing Gluten-free Bread

Anyone familiar with gluten-free baked goods is likely aware of the short time it takes for them to dry out and go stale. While commercially baked bread is improving all the time, when baking at home without preservatives, it is best to store gluten-free bread products as soon as they have cooled from the oven. Storing in an airtight container is generally effective if storing only for 24 hours or so, but if you plan to save the products for much longer, it is best to freeze them as quickly as possible (once cooled). Slice or portion as necessary, then wrap the items in plastic or store in an airtight container to freeze.

Reheating Gluten-free Bread

As it's likely that a fair few of the baked goods you make from this book will be stored to preserve the taste and texture, it's important to reheat them in a way that promotes this as well. I find that the microwave is the most effective method. Wrap the baked item in paper towel or a clean dish towel and then lightly pat some water around the outside (this prevents it from drying out). Reheat using the defrost setting on your microwave for 3–4 minutes or at normal temperature for 1–2 minutes (checking halfway). Allow to cool slightly in the paper towel or dish towel before consuming. If reheating in the oven, wrap in aluminium foil and reheat at 120°C (50°F) for approximately 10 minutes.

Making Breadcrumbs

If you do find yourself with some stale pieces of either the white or brown bread included in this chapter, don't throw them out – they both make truly fantastic breadcrumbs that are the closest I've had to panko breadcrumbs since my diagnosis. Just blitz (or even finely grate) the stale bread into shaggy crumbs and then toast them lightly in the oven or a frying pan to dry them out before storing.

Rustic White Bread Loaf

Makes 1 loaf

DAIRY FREE · NUT FREE · SOY FREE · VEGETARIAN

Fun fact: when I made this bread, cut it open and tasted it for the first time, I panicked, thinking I had accidentally 'glutened' myself. I frantically recalled everything I had used, wondering whether I had somehow slipped up and used wheat flour, despite wheat flour not even existing in my kitchen! It just looked, sounded and smelled so much like 'normal' bread, I couldn't believe it.

This loaf has a thick, crunchy crust with a very satisfying crackle as you press on or cut through it. The bread inside is light and fluffy, with none of the gumminess so often present in gluten-free bread. It also tears like regular bread, with strands that slowly stretch and pull apart, unlike the more brittle breaking that gluten-free people are accustomed to. Of course, making gluten-free bread is subject to many of the subtle rules that govern 'regular' bread-making, perhaps to a greater extent as there are more variables involved in the ingredients. Before you tackle this recipe, or indeed, any of the bread recipes in this book, I'd highly recommend reading the information on baking bread in the chapter introduction (page 103).

200 g (7 oz) warm water

2 tbsp caster (superfine) sugar

3½ tsp instant dried yeast

340 g (12 oz) Basic Plain Flour Blend (plus extra, for dusting) (page 11)

5¼ tsp psyllium husk powder

1 tsp xanthan gum

1 tsp GF baking powder

½ tsp salt

½ tbsp caster (superfine) sugar, extra

2 large eggs (90–95 g or 3–3¼ oz without shell)

40 g (1½ oz) neutral oil (such as canola or vegetable)

5–6 ice cubes

1. Weigh the warm water in a medium jug (see page 104 for a note on warm water). Add the sugar, then sprinkle in the yeast. Whisk it well, then cover with a dish towel and set aside somewhere warm (see chapter introduction for suggestions) for 10 minutes.

2. Meanwhile, place the flour, psyllium husk, xanthan gum, baking powder, salt and extra sugar into a large bowl or the bowl of a stand mixer. Stir to combine the dry ingredients.

3. When 10 minutes have passed, the yeast mixture should appear frothy. Add the eggs and oil into the jug. Whisk to combine, then pour the wet ingredients into the bowl with the dry ingredients.

4. Combine the ingredients at medium speed with an electric mixer fitted with dough hooks, or the paddle attachment on a stand mixer. If you do not have an electric mixer, mix well with a wooden spoon. When the dough has come together, it will be very sticky and coat the base and sides of the bowl. At this point, scrape the sides of the bowl with a sturdy spatula or dough scraper and form it into a rough single ball.

→

5. Continue mixing for 2–3 minutes. Initially the dough should clean the sides of the bowl but will begin to stick at the base. If mixing with a wooden spoon, this will take at least 7–8 minutes. Don't be tempted to knead by hand as the dough will be too sticky and you don't want to incorporate more flour at this stage.

6. Lightly grease a second medium-large bowl with oil, then gather the dough together once more with a sturdy spatula or dough scraper. Turn the dough out into the greased bowl, then gently turn the dough over a few times to coat it lightly with oil on all sides. Cover with plastic wrap, then a dish towel, and leave to prove in a warm, draft-free place for an hour.

7. After an hour, lightly dust your work surface with flour (using no more than about 2 tsp of flour). Turn the dough (which should have doubled in size and will resemble a cauliflower) out onto the floured surface. Lightly dust the top of the dough with flour then knead gently by hand for 2–3 minutes until the dough is smooth. It should be slightly sticky but not clinging to your hands and the work surface.

8. Shape the dough into a smooth ball, gathering it at the bottom so that any seams in the dough ball are on the underside. Lightly flour a clean bowl or banneton basket and place the dough top side down into the bowl or basket. Cover loosely with plastic wrap, then a dish towel, and place again in a warm, draft-free spot for the final prove. Let the dough rise for another hour.

9. With about 20 minutes left of the final prove, preheat the oven to 220°C (430°F), leaving the baking tray you'll use for the loaf in the middle rack of the oven to heat too. Also place a second baking tray (with a rim) on the lowest rack of the oven.

10. After an hour, tip the dough onto a sheet of baking paper. Using a small, sharp knife or bread lame (see chapter introduction), score the bread once down the loaf in a gentle arc slightly off-centre.

11. Once scored to your liking, prepare to place the bread in the oven by having the ice cubes directly at hand. Quickly but gently, lift the dough using the baking paper and place it on the preheated tray in the middle of the oven, then immediately put the ice cubes into the heated tray on the lowest rack. Close the oven door straight away.

12. Allow to bake at 220°C (430°F) for 30 minutes, then turn the oven temperature down to 180°C (360°F) and bake for a further 45 minutes. I like to open the oven and rotate the loaf at this point to make sure that it browns evenly. This also helps to bring down the oven temperature.

13. After 45 minutes, the bread loaf should be a rich brown color. Remove from the oven and place on a cooling rack. Allow to cool for at least 2 hours before slicing.

Brown(er) Bread

Makes 1 loaf

Note that this bread isn't as richly brown as a traditional or 'normal' wholegrain or wholemeal loaf. Those breads require whole grains and less starch, which I find results in loaves that can be gummy in texture when baking gluten-free. This loaf is therefore a kind of hybrid loaf with a balance of some wholegrain flour and starch that creates a richer loaf while still maintaining the pleasant bready texture of the Rustic White Bread Loaf recipe.

220 g (8 oz) warm water
1 ½ tbsp caster (superfine) sugar
3 ¾ tsp instant dried yeast
250 g (9oz) Basic Plain Flour Blend (page 11)
30 g (1 oz) buckwheat flour
60 g (2 oz) brown rice flour
6 ¾ tsp psyllium husk powder
1 ½ tsp xanthan gum
1 ¾ tsp GF baking powder
¾ tsp salt
1 ½ tbsp caster (superfine) sugar, extra
2 large eggs (90–95 g or 3–3 ¼ oz without shell)
40 g (1 ½ oz) neutral oil (such as canola or vegetable)
rice flour, for dusting
5–6 ice cubes

1. Weigh the warm water in a medium jug (see page 104 for a note on warm water). Add the sugar, then sprinkle in the yeast. Whisk it well, then cover with a dish towel and set aside somewhere warm (see chapter introduction for suggestions) for 10 minutes.

2. Meanwhile, place the flours, psyllium husk, xanthan gum, baking powder, salt and extra sugar into a large bowl or the bowl of a stand mixer. Stir to combine the dry ingredients.

3. When 10 minutes have passed, the yeast mixture should appear frothy. Crack the eggs into the jug and add the oil. Whisk to combine, then pour the wet ingredients into the bowl with the dry ingredients.

4. Combine the ingredients at medium speed with an electric mixer fitted with dough hooks, or the paddle attachment on a stand mixer. If you do not have an electric mixer, mix well with a wooden spoon. When the dough has come together, it will be very sticky and coat the base and sides of the bowl. At this point, scrape the sides of the bowl with a sturdy spatula or dough scraper and form it into a rough single ball.

5. Continue mixing for 2–3 minutes. Initially the dough should clean the sides of the bowl but will begin to stick at the base. If mixing with a wooden spoon, this will take at least 7–8 minutes. Don't be tempted to knead by hand as the dough will be too sticky and you don't want to incorporate more flour at this stage.

→

6. Lightly grease a second large bowl with oil, then gather the dough together once more with a sturdy spatula or dough scraper. Turn the dough out into the greased bowl, then gently turn the dough over a few times to coat it lightly with oil on all sides. Cover with plastic wrap, then a dish towel, and leave to prove in a warm, draft-free place for an hour.

7. After an hour, lightly dust your work surface with flour (using no more than about 2 tsp of flour). Turn the dough (which should have doubled in size and will resemble a cauliflower) out onto the floured surface. Lightly dust the top of the dough, then knead gently by hand for 2–3 minutes until the dough is smooth. It should be slightly sticky but not clinging to your hands and the work surface.

8. Shape the dough into a smooth ball, gathering it at the bottom so that any seams in the dough ball are on the underside. Lightly flour a clean bowl or banneton basket and place the dough top side down into the bowl or basket. Cover loosely with plastic wrap, then a dish towel, and replace in the warm, draft-free area for the final prove. Let the dough rise for another hour.

9. With about 20 minutes left of the final prove, preheat the oven to 220°C (430°F), leaving the baking tray you'll use for the loaf in the middle rack of the oven to heat too. Also place a second baking tray (with a rim) on the lowest rack of the oven.

10. After an hour, tip the dough onto a sheet of baking paper. Using a small, sharp knife or bread lame (see chapter introduction), score the bread once down the loaf in a gentle arc slightly off-centre.

11. Once scored to your liking, prepare to place the bread in the oven by having the ice cubes directly at hand. Quickly but gently, lift the dough using the baking paper and place it on the preheated tray in the middle of the oven, then immediately put the ice cubes into the heated tray on the lowest rack. Close the oven door straight away.

12. Allow to bake at 220°C (430°F) for 30 minutes, then turn the oven temperature down to 170°C (340°F) and bake for a further 55–60 minutes.

13. After 55–60 minutes, the bread loaf should be a rich brown color. Remove from the oven and place on a cooling rack. Allow to cool for at least 2 hours before slicing.

Everything Bagels

Makes 6

These bagels are everything I've been missing in the years since my diagnosis. They have a delectably crisp layer on the outside encasing a light but chewy centre that looks and tastes like 'normal' bread. My version of the seasoning includes nigella seeds. These are optional, of course, but they add a mild aromatic warmth that complements the bagel and the other seasonings incredibly well. If you're unsure about the nigella seeds, you can always top the majority of the bagels with the seasoning without them and then just add a sprinkle of nigella seeds to the seed mix for the last one. Then you'll know whether you like it for next time!

To store, the bagels are best frozen fresh. As soon as the bagels have cooled, cut them in half horizontally, then seal in plastic and freeze.

270 g (9½ oz) warm water

1 tbsp caster (superfine) sugar

4 tsp instant dried yeast

340 g (12 oz) Basic Plain Flour Blend (page 11)

5¼ tsp psyllium husk powder

1 tsp xanthan gum

1½ tsp GF baking powder

½ tsp salt

2 tsp caster (superfine) sugar, extra

30 g (1 oz) butter, at room temperature

½ tsp bicarbonate soda

2 tbsp molasses

Seasoning

1 tbsp black sesame seeds

2 tbsp white sesame seeds

1 tbsp poppy seeds

½ tbsp salt flakes

½ tbsp onion flakes

½ tbsp garlic granules

½ tsp nigella seeds

1. Weigh the warm water in a medium jug (see page 104 for a note on warm water). Add the sugar, then sprinkle in the yeast. Whisk it well, then cover with a dish towel and set aside somewhere warm (see chapter introduction for suggestions) for 10 minutes.

2. Meanwhile, place the flour, psyllium husk, xanthan gum, baking powder, salt and extra sugar into a large bowl or the bowl of a stand mixer fitted with a paddle attachment. Stir to combine the dry ingredients.

3. When 10 minutes have passed, the yeast mixture should have a thick layer of foam above the water. Tip this mixture into the dry ingredients and start mixing on medium speed. If you do not have an electric mixer, mix vigorously with a wooden spoon.

4. When the majority of the dough is starting to come together (with some dry crumbs and pieces in the bottom of the bowl), scrape down the bowl and add the butter. Continue mixing on medium speed for 3–4 minutes in a mixer or 5–6 minutes of mixing by hand. The dough should come together in a single ball, cleaning the sides of the bowl.

→

←

5. Continue to mix for 4–5 minutes, until the dough gets sticky again and starts sticking to the base of the mixing bowl. If mixing by hand, turn it onto a clean surface (do not dust with flour) and knead vigorously by hand for 6–7 minutes. The dough should get sticky again to the point that it is hard to handle as it clings to your fingers. Do not be tempted to add flour.

6. Lightly grease another medium-large bowl with oil, then gather the dough and place it in the bowl in one rough ball. Gently turn the dough over a few times to coat it lightly with oil on all sides. Cover with plastic wrap, then a dish towel, and leave to prove in a warm, draft-free place for an hour. While you wait, line a large baking tray with parchment paper.

7. After an hour, the dough should have doubled in size. Tip it onto a clean work surface and knead it by hand for about a minute until smooth and pliable.

8. Divide the dough into six equal pieces weighing approximately 115 g (4 oz) each. Working with one piece at a time, knead them gently then roll them into neat balls by cupping your hand over the dough and moving in a circular motion against the work surface.

9. Once a smooth ball has formed, use your finger to poke a hole through the centre of the ball. Keep your finger in the ball with your fingertip touching the work surface and move gently in a circular motion to widen the hole in the centre. This is a less common technique as bagels are traditionally rolled into logs and then looped into a circular shape, but as gluten-free dough doesn't stretch as readily as 'normal' dough, I find this method more effective. Make sure the hole you create is at least 6 cm (2½ in) wide, otherwise it will close up during baking.

10. Once shaped, place the bagels on the prepared baking tray. Lightly moisten your finger and dab some water over the top of the bagels. Cover loosely with plastic wrap, then a dish towel and return the tray to the proving area for 2 hours.

11. While you wait, combine the seasoning ingredients in a shallow bowl or rimmed plate.

12. With about 15 minutes left of the final prove, preheat your oven to 220°C (430°F). Select a large pot that can fit two or three of the bagels comfortably side by side, fill it with 2 litres (68 fl oz) of water and bring it to the boil. Add the bicarbonate of soda and the molasses.

13. Once the bagels have finished proving, gently transfer two or three of them to the boiling water mixture. Leave them for 30 seconds, then flip the bagels and leave for another 30 seconds. Scoop the bagels out with a slotted spoon and allow to drain slightly on a cooling rack. Repeat with the rest of the bagels.

14. When the boiled bagels have cooled just enough to be handled (they should still be very moist), dunk them into the seasoning mixture to coat one side.

15. Place a clean piece of baking paper onto the baking tray and place the bagels (seasoned side up) on the tray, spacing them 4–5 cm (1½–2 in) apart.

16. Bake in the oven for 20–22 minutes, rotating the tray halfway through cooking, then remove the oven tray. Allow the bagels to sit on the baking tray for 5 minutes before transferring to a cooling rack. Let the bagels cool completely before cutting and serving.

Sweet White Bread Dough

Makes 1 portion

This recipe is a total game changer for the gluten-free world of bread! It's a dough that creates a squishy, soft bread that pulls apart like the bread you might remember from your pre-GF days and is a base for many recipes in this book, both sweet and savory. There are so many potential uses for this that I couldn't possibly include them all, but rest assured that once you've mastered this dough, the whole wide world of soft bread opens up to you – from cinnamon rolls to stuffed naan and everything in between. Note that the only application this dough is not great for is for making one singular loaf. It is best when divided into smaller buns or pieces that are then braided or layered.

200 g (7 oz) warm water
30 g (1 oz) caster (superfine) sugar
1 tbsp instant dried yeast
280 g (10 oz) Basic Plain Flour Blend (page 11)
4 tsp psyllium husk powder
1 tsp xanthan gum
1 tsp GF baking powder
½ tsp salt
30 g (1 oz) caster (superfine) sugar, extra
2 eggs
40 g (1½ oz) butter, at room temperature

1. Weigh the warm water in a medium jug or bowl. Add the sugar and sprinkle in the yeast. Whisk well, cover with a dish towel and set aside somewhere warm for 10 minutes.

2. Meanwhile, measure the dry ingredients into a large mixing bowl or the bowl of a stand mixer.

3. After 10 minutes, the yeast mixture should have bloomed, creating a thick layer of foam on top of the water. Crack the eggs into the yeast mixture, beat it lightly and add it to your mixing bowl.

4. Bring the dough together using the paddle attachment of your stand mixer on medium-low speed or, if kneading by hand, a spoon or sturdy spatula. When all the dry ingredients have been moistened so there is not much flour left on the sides or bottom of the bowl, add the butter and incorporate into the dough.

5. Knead in the stand mixer (on medium speed) for 5–6 minutes, stopping two or three times to scrape down the sides of the bowl and ensuring no flour is clumped beneath the dough in the bottom. This dough will be wetter than a traditional dough and therefore can't really be kneaded by hand on a kitchen surface. Instead, keep the dough inside the bowl and stir with a sturdy spoon or spatula (this will take approximately 10 minutes of hard mixing).

6. When the dough is ready it will be very sticky but smooth, and you should be able to use a dough scraper or spatula to scrape it from the inside of the bowl into a single ball. Transfer to a large, lightly greased bowl.

7. Lightly oil your hands and turn the dough ball over in the bowl a few times so that it is lightly greased all over. You should now be able to pick it up without it sticking to your hands and shape it into a reasonably uniform ball. Don't fold it over itself at this stage – the aim is not to incorporate fat into the dough but to simply make it workable. Cover the bowl with plastic wrap, then a dish towel, then place it in a warm, draft-free space in your house for an hour.

8. After an hour, the dough should have doubled in size. Turn it onto a lightly floured work surface and knead it gently with your hands to remove the air bubbles that have formed. You do not want to incorporate too much flour into the dough, just enough to be able to knead and shape it gently.

9. After kneading for about a minute, the dough should be smooth and malleable. It's now ready to be rolled and shaped according to the instructions specific to the recipe you're making.

Garlic Parmesan Loaf

I had never seen a pull-apart loaf like this prior to being gluten-free, and now I feel as though I see them everywhere so of course I had to make my own version. This is made by dividing my Sweet White Bread Dough into small pieces, lathering each one in the garlic butter parmesan mixture, and then stacking the pieces together into a loaf tin. Once baked, it holds its loaf shape but you can pull the pieces off the loaf almost as though it's been pre-sliced. It's great to share, but don't offer to share with too many people because it'll vanish *very* quickly!

1 portion of Sweet White Bread Dough (page 119)
6 garlic cloves
120 g (4 ½ oz) butter, at room temperature
1 ½ tbsp parsley, finely chopped
¼ tsp salt
⅛ tsp cracked black pepper
60 g (2 oz) parmesan, finely grated
1 egg yolk and 1 tbsp single cream, for egg wash

1. Prepare the dough according to directions on page 119. During the first hour-long prove, grease and line a deep 22 x 12 cm (9 x 5 in) loaf tin and make the garlic butter filling.

2. Peel and mince the garlic and add it to the butter. Add the parsley, salt, pepper and parmesan. Mix well until fully combined, then set aside.

3. After the first hour-long prove, tip the dough onto a lightly floured surface and knead it gently until smooth.

4. Roll the dough out into a long log and divide it into 12 equal pieces. Working with one piece at a time, form a neat ball, then press it flat and roll it out slightly until it is roughly rectangular in shape and about 10 x 12 cm (4 x 5 in).

5. Spread the flattened dough generously with some of the garlic butter mixture, then place in one end of the loaf tin. It will help to stand the loaf tin upright so that one of the shorter ends is flat to your work surface. Place the flattened dough (uncoated side down) on this end to form the first of the stack that will fill the loaf tin.

6. Repeat with the rest of the dough and garlic butter mixture, turning the loaf tin the right way up as you progress. Place the last piece of dough with the coated side facing inwards towards the centre of the loaf. The pieces of dough should fit comfortably in the tin with some room for them to expand during proving and baking. The result will be a layered loaf full of garlic, butter and cheese that can be pulled apart by the slice once cooked.

7. Cover the loaf tin loosely with plastic wrap, then a dish towel, and place back in a warm, draft-free spot for a final 45-minute prove.

8. With about 15 minutes of this prove remaining, preheat your oven to 160°C (320°F) and prepare the egg wash by combining the egg yolk and cream in a small bowl.

9. After proving, uncover the loaf and use a pastry brush to coat it gently in the egg wash. Place the baking tray in the preheated oven to bake for 30–35 minutes.

10. The loaf should have increased in size by at least 50 per cent and be golden brown in color. Allow to cool slightly before serving.

Cheesy Dinner Rolls

Makes 12

This is another recipe inspired by some of the bread products I used to be able to eat in Japan as a kid. Any supermarket or convenience store will sell these small, shiny brown buns that are beautifully soft and stuffed with custard, peanut butter, cream cheese and any number of other delicious fillings. The cheese ones were always my favorite and to my absolute delight, I've found I can achieve a *very* similar result by stuffing portions of my Sweet White Bread Dough with balls of soft cheese.

1 portion of Sweet White Bread Dough (page 119)
12 pieces of soft cheese (like Laughing Cow or similar)
1 egg yolk and 1 tbsp single cream, for egg wash
sesame seeds, optional

1. Prepare the dough according to directions on page 119. During the first hour-long prove, line a baking tray with parchment paper and prepare the soft cheese pieces by rolling them into neat balls (wet or grease your hands slightly to make this easier). Set them aside.

2. After the hour-long prove, tip the dough onto a lightly floured surface and knead it gently until smooth.

3. Roll the dough out into a long log and divide it into 12 (you can make fewer buns if you'd like them slightly larger). Working with one piece at a time, form a neat ball, then press it flat and roll it out slightly into a roughly circular shape about 10 cm (4 in) in diameter.

4. Place one of the cheese balls in the centre of the dough, then gather the edges together, sealing the cheese inside. Pinch the dough together to close the seams well, then place the ball seam side down on your work surface. Cup your hand over the ball and roll it in a circular motion to form a perfect bun shape.

5. Place the shaped bun onto the prepared baking tray and repeat with the rest of the dough.

6. Cover the tray loosely with plastic wrap, then a dish towel, and place back in a warm, draft-free spot for a final 45-minute prove.

7. With about 15 minutes of this prove remaining, preheat your oven to 160°C (320°F) and prepare the egg wash by combining the egg yolk and cream in a small bowl.

8. After proving, uncover the buns and use a pastry brush to coat them gently in the egg wash, then sprinkle with sesame seeds if desired.

9. Place the tray in the preheated oven to bake for 20–22 minutes. The buns should have increased in size by at least 50 per cent and be golden brown in color.

10. Allow to cool slightly before serving.

Pigs in Blankets

Makes 20

These are my version of Chinese hot dog buns, another popular bready treat readily available in Japan that I indulged in as often as possible prior to my celiac diagnosis. They are made by wrapping little pork sausages in strands of soft and sweet bread dough. If you can find GF Japanese pork sausages, I highly recommend you use them, but as they're not easy to find, use whatever is available to you.

20 small GF hot dog sausages
½ portion of Sweet White Bread Dough (page 119)
1 egg yolk and 1 tbsp single cream, for egg wash
sesame seeds, to garnish

1. Line two baking trays with parchment paper and set aside.

2. Prepare the dough according to directions on page 119. After the first hour-long prove, tip the dough onto a lightly floured surface and knead gently until smooth.

3. Roll the dough out into a long log and divide into 20 pieces. Working with one piece at a time, roll it out again into a smaller, narrower rope about 25 cm (10 in) long.

4. Take one hot dog and wrap a rope around it three or four times, or until you run out of dough. Ideally, leave about 1 cm (½ in) of sausage peeping out from either end so that it is not completely encased in bread after baking. Try to start and finish wrapping the dough on the same side of the hot dog so that you can then place that side down onto a lined baking tray. This will prevent the dough from unravelling as it cooks. Repeat with the rest of the hot dogs and bread dough.

5. Once all the hot dogs have been rolled and placed 3–4 cm (about 1½ in) apart on the baking trays, cover loosely with plastic wrap, then a dish towel, and place back in a warm, draft-free area for a final 45-minute prove.

6. With about 15 minutes of this prove remaining, preheat your oven to 160°C (320°F) and prepare the egg wash by combining the egg yolk and cream in a small bowl.

7. After proving, uncover the buns and use a pastry brush to coat them in the egg wash. The buns will be very delicate so be gentle! Top them with a sprinkle of sesame seeds.

8. Place the tray in the preheated oven to bake for 16–18 minutes. The buns should have increased in size by at least 50 per cent and be golden brown in color.

9. Allow to cool slightly before serving.

Pan-fried Beef Bao

Makes 10–12

Bao buns are one of those foods that I had barely been acquainted with before becoming gluten-free, and that really disappoints me! That's why I've put a lot of effort into making a GF version. While I'm still experimenting with steamed bao, these are a wonderful option for filling with any kind of braised or barbequed meats. They're pillowy and soft and get a lovely texture on the outside from frying in the pan. Be sure to start the filling early as this needs to be made in advance of the bread dough.

Beef filling

- 500 g (1 lb 2 oz) chuck steak or other beef cut for stewing
- 1 tbsp GF cornstarch
- ½ tsp white pepper
- 1 tbsp neutral oil
- 1 brown onion, sliced
- 2–3 garlic cloves, finely chopped
- 7–8 cm (3 in) piece of ginger, sliced
- 2 tbsp GF Chinese cooking wine (use cooking sake if Shaoxing or similar is unavailable)
- 1 ½ tbsp GF soy sauce
- 1 tbsp GF oyster sauce
- 200 ml (7 fl oz) water
- 1 tbsp caster (superfine) sugar
- ½ cinnamon stick
- 3 cloves
- ½ star anise
- 2 dried chillies (optional)
- 1 tsp sesame oil
- ½ tsp salt (adjust to taste)

Dough

- 130 ml (4 ½ fl oz) water
- 130 ml (4 ½ fl oz) milk
- 2 tbsp caster (superfine) sugar, divided
- 3 tsp instant dried yeast
- 240 g (8 ½ oz) Basic Plain Flour Blend (page 11)
- 2 ¼ tsp psyllium husk powder
- ½ tsp xanthan gum
- ⅔ tsp GF baking powder
- ⅔ tsp salt
- 2 tbsp neutral oil
- rice flour, extra (to dust)
- 2 tbsp neutral oil, extra (for frying)
- 4 tsp white or black sesame seeds, to garnish (optional)

Beef filling

1. Chop the steak into 3–4 cm (about 1 ½ in) chunks. Coat lightly with the cornstarch and season the chunks on all sides with the white pepper. Heat the oil in a cast-iron saucepan or the pot of a slow cooker or pressure cooker. Add the beef and sear on all sides.

2. Add the onion, garlic and ginger and cook until fragrant. Add the cooking wine, soy sauce and oyster sauce and turn to coat all the meat. Add the rest of the ingredients, stir to combine. If cooking on the stove, place the lid on the saucepan, reduce the heat to low and simmer for 2–2.5 hours, or until the meat is tender and falling apart. You may need to add some extra water to maintain a stew-like consistency. Alternatively, slow-cook or pressure-cook until the meat is tender.

→

3. When the beef is fork-tender, remove the lid from the saucepan or cooking appliance and increase heat to medium-high, bringing the braising liquid to a simmer. Allow to simmer for 5–10 minutes, until the liquid in the pot has reduced by half and thickened slightly.

4. Take off the heat and remove the beef from the stew with a slotted spoon. Place in a bowl and cut or shred the meat into small pieces. Add 2–3 tbsp of the braising liquid and any onion or garlic pieces that are still visible into the bowl with the meat and stir to combine. The mixture should resemble a pie filling, with just enough sauce to coat and combine the meat. Allow to cool, then cover and store in the fridge while you make the dough.

Dough

1. To make the dough, measure the water and milk into a medium microwave-safe jug. Heat in the microwave for 20–30 seconds or until the liquid is warm (but not hot) to the touch. Add half the sugar, stir, then sprinkle the yeast over the mixture and whisk well to combine. Cover with a dish towel and set aside for 10 minutes. Meanwhile, measure the dry ingredients (including the rest of the sugar) into a mixing bowl or the bowl of a stand mixer.

2. When the yeast mixture is foamy, add the oil to the jug, stir, then pour the wet ingredients into the dry. Combine with the paddle attachment on a stand mixer or a sturdy wooden spoon or spatula if mixing by hand.

3. Continue to mix well (medium speed on a mixer) until the dough is smooth, soft and pliable. Oil your hands and shape the dough into a ball before placing it in a fresh, lightly greased bowl. Cover with plastic wrap and a dish towel, then allow it to prove in a warm, draft-free place for an hour.

4. After an hour, tip the dough onto a clean work surface and knead gently to remove excess air pockets. Dust with rice flour very sparingly, using only a pinch as necessary if the dough is overly sticky or difficult to handle. Divide the dough into 10 or 12 portions (depending on the size of the bun you'd like to make) then, working one at a time, flatten each piece into a thick disc. Use a rolling pin to roll the dough only around the outer edges – this part of the disc should be thinner because it will be gathered at the top of the bun. Leave the centre of the disc at least 1 cm (½ in) thick.

5. Place a spoonful of the beef mixture into the centre of the disc, then lift the edges of the dough and gather them on top of the filling, pinching and folding as necessary to enclose the meat. Seal the top well, then pull off any excess dough beyond the point where the bun has come together. Turn the bun upside down, then pat down gently with your hand to form the bun into a thick disc once more.

6. Repeat with the remaining dough, then space the buns out on a plate or tray, cover loosely with plastic wrap, then a dish towel, and place back in a warm, draft-free place to prove for 45 minutes.

7. Heat the cooking oil in a large frying pan with a lid over medium-low heat. If using the sesame seeds, place them in a shallow bowl and gently dip one side of each bun into the seeds before placing them (seed side down) into the frying pan.

8. Place the lid on and cook for 5–6 minutes, checking occasionally that the buns aren't burning, then flip the buns to brown on the other side. When the buns are golden, remove the lid from the pan and allow any excess moisture to evaporate as the buns turn a little darker and slightly crisp on the bottom. Remove from the heat and serve hot with a sauce of your choice if desired. I like to drizzle mine with chilli oil.

Fingerbuns

Makes 6

These are a bit of an Australian delicacy – a fancy iteration of the modest 'fairy bread' that would appear at every kid's birthday party, picnic, or school function (if we were lucky!) For those unfamiliar with it, fairy bread is simply slices of buttered white bread topped with sprinkles, but it's somehow delicious and satisfying. With or without the nostalgia, anyone is bound to enjoy the combination of soft white bread and the sweet crunch of sprinkles.

1 portion of Sweet White Bread Dough (page 119)
1 egg yolk
1 tbsp single cream

Glaze (optional)

50 ml (1 ¾ fl oz) water
50 g (1 ¾ oz) caster (superfine) sugar

Icing

150 g (5 ½ oz) butter (at room temperature)
150 g (5 ½ oz) GF icing sugar
1 tsp vanilla bean paste (or extract)
⅛ tsp salt
½ cup multicolored GF sprinkles

1. Prepare the dough according to instructions on page 119. After the first hour-long prove, tip the dough onto a lightly floured surface and knead it gently until smooth.

2. Roll the dough into a log, then divide it evenly into six pieces. Working with one piece at a time, knead the balls of dough and flatten them into discs on your work surface. Then roll them up from one edge, forming small rolled logs.

3. Place them on baking trays lined with parchment paper spaced 2–3 cm (about 1 in) apart. A baguette tray also works to create perfectly rounded buns, but this isn't essential.

4. Cover the baking tray loosely with plastic wrap, then a dish towel, and place the buns back in a warm, draft-free spot. Allow them to prove for a total of 45 minutes, but preheat your oven to 160°C (320°F) before they've finished proving so that it is hot enough when the buns are ready to bake.

5. Prepare an egg wash by combining the egg yolk and cream in a small bowl.

6. After 45 minutes, uncover the buns and use a pastry brush to coat them in the egg wash. The buns will be very delicate so be gentle!

7. Place the baking tray in the preheated oven to bake for 18–20 minutes. The buns should have increased in size by at least 50 per cent and be a rich golden brown.

8. While the buns cool, make the glaze. This is an optional step – the glaze is a simple sugar syrup that will add a glossy sheen and delectable stickiness to the buns. Simply combine the water and sugar in a small saucepan and heat until the sugar has dissolved completely.

9. Use a pastry brush to glaze the buns with the syrup while they're still hot.

10. When the buns have almost cooled completely, make the icing. Using an electric beater or stand mixer, whisk the butter until pale and fluffy. Sift in the icing sugar, add the vanilla and salt, and continue whisking until the sugar granules have completely dissolved. This will likely take about 10 minutes.

11. Top each bun generously with the icing, smoothing it into an even layer, then either scatter the multicolored sprinkles over the top of each bun or place the sprinkles into a shallow bowl and dip the buns into them, icing side down, to coat the buns evenly. The buns are best served fresh.

Pistachio Cardamom Scrolls

Makes 8

This is one of my all-time favorite recipes. Not just in this book, not just since I was diagnosed with celiac disease. One of my favorite recipes *ever*. These scrolls were inspired by a type of Swedish cinnamon bun my grandmother used to make. They were stuffed with almond paste and had cardamom and cinnamon inside, combining to make the warmest, most satisfying buns I thought I'd ever eat (that recipe can also be found on page 141). I decided to tweak these to pair pistachio with the cardamom instead, which I think is an almost unbeatable flavor combination. The result is a sweet but complex filling inside a soft and fluffy bread dough, something I never imagined I'd be able to eat let alone make myself in the early years of my celiac diagnosis.

70 g (2 ½ oz) shelled raw pistachios (unsalted)
15 g (½ oz) caster (superfine) sugar
20 g (¾ oz) egg white (about half of 1 egg white)
1 portion of Sweet White Bread Dough (page 119)

Cardamom sugar filling

25 g (1 oz) caster (superfine) sugar
¾ tsp cardamom
¼ tsp cinnamon
50 g (1 ¾ oz) butter

Egg wash

1 egg yolk
1 tbsp single cream
50 g (1 ¾ oz) sugar crystals, to decorate (optional)

Glaze (optional)

50 ml (1 ¾ fl oz) water
50 g (1 ¾ oz) sugar

1. Place the pistachios and sugar into the canister of a food processor and blitz until it resembles fine crumbs. Add to a small bowl with the egg white and mix until combined. Gather the mixture into a ball and spoon it onto a sheet of plastic wrap. Wrap it tightly to form a small, thick log and freeze it solid.

2. Prepare the dough according to instructions on page 119.

3. During the first hour-long prove, prepare the cardamom sugar filling by combining the dry ingredients in a small bowl. Weigh out the butter but keep it separate from the sugar mixture. Set these aside. Next, line two baking trays with parchment paper.

4. After an hour, the dough should have doubled in size. Turn it onto a lightly floured work surface and knead it gently with your hands to remove the air bubbles that have formed. You do not want to incorporate too much flour into the dough, just enough to be able to knead and shape it gently.

5. After kneading for about a minute, the dough should be smooth and malleable. Roll it out onto your work surface (a silicon mat may help to prevent it sticking to your kitchen bench) until it forms a rectangle approximately 28 x 45 cm (11 x 18 in). Position the dough so that the rectangle is horizontal in front of you and make a lightly indented line down the centre so that you can see a clear division between the left and right halves.

→

←

6. Use a spatula to gently spread the butter evenly over the left half of the dough rectangle. Sift the cardamom sugar mixture over the same half of the dough rectangle to form an even layer over the butter.

7. Take the pistachio paste from the freezer, unwrap it and grate it over the cardamom sugar and butter. Distribute the pistachio paste as evenly as possible over the left side of the rectangle, using your hands to press the grated paste gently into the butter and spiced sugar.

8. Gently lift the bare right half of the dough rectangle over the left half. Align the edges as closely as you can, then use a rolling pin to gently press the halves together as you roll it out slightly, not expanding this new rectangle by more than 2 or 3 cm (about 1 in). The dough should now be positioned so that one of the shorter ends of the rectangle is closest to you and the folded seam runs up the right side of the new rectangle.

9. Divide the dough into eight by making seven cuts approximately 4 cm (1½ in) apart parallel to the shorter edges of the rectangle. You will now have eight narrow rectangular pieces of dough that have a single layer of filling and are joined by a seam on one end.

10. Cut up the middle of each rectangle towards the seam, but don't cut through it. Leave about 2 cm (¾ in) uncut, meaning that you will now have two 'legs' of dough that are attached at the top by the seam. Gently twist those 'legs' around each other to form a spiral, then roll the spiral in on itself with the joined seam at the centre. Tuck the ends of the twisted 'legs' underneath the main part of the bun, then place on one of the lined baking trays.

11. Repeat with each piece of dough, cutting down the centre, twisting the 'legs' together, then rolling them into a spiral and placing them on the baking tray. When all eight buns have been shaped, cover loosely with plastic wrap, then a dish towel, and place them back in a warm, draft-free spot. Allow them to prove for a total of 45 minutes, but preheat your oven to 160°C (320°F) before they've finished proving so that it is hot enough when the buns are ready to bake.

12. Prepare the egg wash by combining the egg yolk and cream in a small bowl. After 45 minutes, uncover the buns and use a pastry brush to coat them in the egg wash. The buns will be very delicate so be gentle! Top the buns with a generous sprinkle of sugar crystals (if using), then place them in the preheated oven to bake for 16–18 minutes. The buns should have increased in size by at least 50 per cent and be a rich golden brown.

13. While the buns cool, make the glaze. This is an optional step – the glaze is a simple sugar syrup that will add a glossy sheen and delectable stickiness to the buns. Simply combine the water and sugar in a small saucepan and heat until the sugar has dissolved completely.

14. Use a pastry brush to glaze the buns with the sugar syrup while they're still hot. Allow the buns to cool slightly before serving.

Blueberry Custard Buns

Makes 9

My dad loves bread and blueberries, respectively, but he doesn't generally like sweets. These were an attempt to win him over and I'm happy to say it worked! They're not overly sweet, even with the custard, so they're a great accompaniment to afternoon tea.

1 portion of Sweet White Bread Dough (page 119)

Custard filling

2 egg yolks
1 ½ tbsp caster (superfine) sugar
1 ½ tbsp GF cornstarch
120 ml (4 fl oz) milk
80 ml (2 ½ fl oz) single cream
½ tsp vanilla bean paste (or extract)
⅛ tsp salt

Egg wash

1 egg yolk, extra
1 tbsp single cream, extra

Garnish

100 g (3 ½ oz) fresh blueberries
50 ml (1 ¾ fl oz) water
50 g (1 ¾ oz) sugar

1. Prepare the dough according to directions on page 119. During the first hour-long prove, line a large baking tray with parchment paper and set aside. Then make the custard filling.

2. Combine the egg yolks, sugar and cornstarch in a medium mixing bowl and whisk well until pale and creamy.

3. In a small saucepan, add the milk, cream, vanilla and salt. Stir regularly until it's just simmering, then trickle it over the egg yolk mixture, whisking constantly. Once combined, tip the mixture into a clean saucepan and place it over a medium-low heat, whisking consistently.

4. As it starts to thicken, reduce the heat and continue to whisk well until it has become a thick custard. Remove from the heat and pour it into a shallow bowl to cool.

5. After the first hour-long prove, tip the dough onto a lightly floured surface and knead it gently until smooth. Roll the dough out into a long log and divide it into nine equal pieces. Working with one piece at a time, roll them into neat balls by cupping your hand over the dough and moving in a circular motion against the work surface.

6. Use a rolling pin to gently flatten the balls of dough into thick discs, then space them out onto the baking tray, leaving 4–5 cm (1 ½–2 in) between each bun. When all the buns have been shaped, cover the baking tray loosely with plastic wrap, then a dish towel, and place back in a warm, draft-free spot for a final 45-minute prove.

→

7. With about 15 minutes of this prove remaining, preheat your oven to 160°C (320°F) and prepare the egg wash by combining the extra egg yolk and cream in a small bowl.

8. After proving, uncover the baking tray and use the base of a very small bowl or narrow glass to gently indent the centre of each bun. Push the implement down until you can feel the baking tray underneath but try not to tear the dough.

9. Spoon custard into the indent of each bun, filling them three-quarters full. If desired, drop one or two blueberries into each indent as well (these will go jammy as they're cooked) or simply leave all the blueberries for garnishing later.

10. Use a pastry brush to coat the buns gently in the egg wash, avoiding the custard centres.

11. Place the baking tray in the preheated oven to bake for 18–20 minutes. The buns should have increased in size by at least 50 per cent and be golden brown in color.

12. While the buns cool, make the glaze. This is an optional step – the glaze is a simple sugar syrup that will add a glossy sheen and delectable stickiness to the buns. Simply combine the water and sugar in a small saucepan and heat until the sugar has dissolved completely.

13. Use a pastry brush to glaze the buns lightly with the sugar syrup while they're still hot, again avoiding the custard centres.

14. Allow the buns to cool slightly, then garnish with fresh blueberries and serve while warm.

Almond Cinnamon Buns (*Kanelbullar*)

Makes 8–10

SOY FREE   VEGETARIAN

I'm very sentimental about these buns because the first ones I ever had were lovingly made for me by my Swedish grandmother, known to me as *Farmor* (meaning mother of my father). She passed away when I was a teenager and as she lived in Sweden, I wasn't able to spend anywhere near as much time with her as I would have liked. Baking these with her at four or five years old is a cherished memory and I wish she could have seen me grow up to immortalize them in my cookbook. They're not perfectly traditional, especially as they're now gluten-free, but they taste just like the ones I used to eat fresh and warm in my *farmor*'s kitchen.

115 g (4 oz) almond meal

1 egg white

1 portion of Sweet White Bread Dough (page 119)

50 g (1 ¾ oz) butter, at room temperature

50 g (1 ¾ oz) soft brown sugar

1 tbsp cinnamon

Egg wash

1 egg yolk

1 tbsp single cream

50 g (1 ¾ oz) sugar crystals, to decorate (optional)

Glaze (optional)

50 ml (1 ¾ fl oz) water

50 g (1 ¾ oz) sugar

1. Start by making the almond paste for the filling. Combine the almond meal and egg white in a small bowl and mix very well. Gather the mixture into a ball and spoon it onto a sheet of plastic wrap. Wrap it tightly to form a small, thick log and freeze it solid.

2. Prepare the dough according to the instructions on page 119.

3. After the first hour-long prove, the dough should have doubled in size. Turn it onto a lightly floured work surface and knead it gently with your hands to remove the air bubbles that have formed. You do not want to incorporate too much flour into the dough, just enough to be able to knead and shape it gently.

4. After kneading for about a minute, the dough should be smooth and malleable. Roll it out onto your work surface (a silicon mat may help to prevent it sticking to your kitchen bench) until it forms a rectangle approximately 26 x 40 cm (10 x 16 in). Position the rectangle of dough horizontally in front of you.

5. Use a spatula to gently spread the butter for the filling evenly over the left and middle thirds of the dough. Sprinkle the brown sugar as evenly as possible over the butter.

6. Take the almond paste from the freezer, unwrap it and grate it over the sugar and butter. Distribute the almond paste as evenly as possible, using your hands to press the grated paste gently into the butter and sugar. Sift the cinnamon evenly over the filling.

→

7. Working carefully, lift the right-hand third of the dough rectangle over the filled middle third. Press down gently to seal the filling in place. Then lift the folded portion over the final third, lining the edges of the dough up as neatly as you can. Folding the dough this way creates three layers and prevents the filling from falling out as the dough is folded.

8. Use a rolling pin to gently press the layers together as you roll it out slightly. You should be able to increase the size of the new rectangle by about 30 per cent before the filling starts to show through the dough. Be careful not to roll it too thin as the dough will then break during shaping.

9. Using a sharp knife or pizza wheel, cut 1.5–2 cm (½–¾ in) strips along the length of the rectangle. Gently lift the end of one of these strips and wrap it around two or three of your fingers. Wrap it one and a half times (stretch the dough as little as possible – gluten-free dough is not as elastic as regular dough and will break), then take it off your fingers and change the direction of the wrap to go around the middle of the loop you created. Do this carefully, keeping the layers of dough together as much as possible.

10. There should be enough dough to wrap around the loop once and finish on the underside of the bun. Tuck the end into the bottom of the knot you've created and place it on one of the prepared baking trays. Repeat with the rest of the strips of dough, spacing the buns 5–6 cm (2–2½ in) apart on the baking tray.

11. When all the buns have been shaped, cover loosely with plastic wrap, then a dish towel, and place them back in a warm, draft-free spot. Allow them to prove for a total of 45 minutes, but preheat your oven to 160°C (320°F) before they've finished proving so that it is hot enough when the buns are ready to bake.

12. Prepare the egg wash by combining the egg yolk and cream in a small bowl. After proving, uncover the buns and use a pastry brush to coat them in the egg wash. The buns will be very delicate so be gentle! Top the buns with a generous sprinkle of sugar crystals (if using), then place them in the preheated oven to bake for 16–18 minutes. The buns should have increased in size by at least 50 per cent and be a rich golden brown.

13. While the buns cool, make the glaze. This is an optional step – the glaze is a simple sugar syrup that will add a glossy sheen and delectable stickiness to the buns. Simply combine the water and sugar in a small saucepan and heat until the sugar has dissolved completely.

14. Use a pastry brush to lightly glaze the buns with the sugar syrup while they're still hot. Allow the buns to cool slightly before serving.

Yeasted Doughnuts

Makes 8–10

Fried yeasted doughnuts have been something of a holy grail to me since I started baking gluten-free. I tried and failed with many recipes, and even the recipes that worked weren't nearly as satisfying as I hoped they would be. When I made these, I was shocked at how well they mimicked regular doughnuts and I've been itching to share the recipe ever since. These make for perfect O-shaped versions or the filled doughnuts that are piped with various flavorings. I've included my three favorite fillings below as options: salted caramel, custard and strawberry jam.

100 g (3½ oz) warm water
1 tbsp caster (superfine) sugar
1½ tsp yeast
170 g (6 oz) Basic Plain Flour Blend (page 11)
2¼ tsp psyllium husk powder
½ tsp xanthan gum
⅔ tsp GF baking powder
¼ tsp salt
1 egg
20 g (¾ oz) butter, at room temperature
100 g (3½ oz) caster (superfine) sugar, to coat
15 g (½ oz) cinnamon, to coat (optional)
1.5–2 L (51–68 fl oz) neutral oil, for frying (rice bran, sunflower seed, canola or vegetable)

1. Weigh the warm water into a medium jug or bowl. Add the sugar and sprinkle over the yeast. Whisk well, then cover with a dish towel and set aside for 10 minutes.

2. Meanwhile, measure the dry ingredients into your mixing bowl (I use the bowl of my stand mixer).

3. After 10 minutes, the yeast mixture should have bloomed, meaning there should be a thick layer of foam formed on the water. Crack the egg into the yeast mixture, beat it lightly and add it to your mixing bowl. Bring the dough together using the paddle attachment of your stand mixer on medium-low speed or, if kneading by hand, a sturdy spoon or spatula.

4. When the dough has combined, scrape down the sides of the bowl and add the butter. If mixing by hand, continue stirring vigorously for about 10 minutes. If using a stand mixer, continue to mix on medium speed for 5–6 minutes, scraping the dough away from the sides of the bowl two or three times.

5. When the dough is ready it will be very sticky but smooth, and you should be able to use a spatula or dough scraper to scrape it from the inside of the bowl into a single ball. Transfer to a large, greased bowl.

6. Turn the dough over in the bowl a few times so that the dough ball is lightly greased all over. You should now be able to pick it up without it sticking to your hands and shape it into a reasonably uniform ball. Don't fold it over itself at this stage – the aim is not to incorporate fat into the dough but to simply make it workable. Cover the bowl with plastic wrap, then a dish towel, and place it in a warm, draft-free spot for an hour.

7. Meanwhile, line a baking tray with parchment paper and set aside, and then make your desired fillings (see my suggestions for custard, jam or salted caramel doughnuts). Also prepare the doughnut coating, placing the sugar in a shallow bowl and mixing in the cinnamon if using.

8. After an hour, the dough should have doubled in size. Turn it onto a lightly floured work surface and knead it gently with your hands to remove any air bubbles that have formed. You do not want to incorporate too much flour into the dough, just enough to be able to knead and shape it gently. After kneading for about a minute, the dough should be smooth and malleable. Roll it out onto your work surface (a silicon mat may help to prevent it sticking to your kitchen bench) until it is approximately 2 cm (¾ in) thick.

→

9. Use a round 7–8 cm (3 in) cookie cutter to cut out circles of dough and place them on the prepared baking tray (use a smaller cookie cutter to cut holes out of the centre of the doughnuts if you wish to make unfilled doughnuts). Cover the tray of doughnuts loosely with plastic wrap, then a dish towel, and place them back in a warm, draft-free spot. Allow them to prove for a total of 35 minutes.

10. While the doughnuts are proving, prepare oil for deep-frying. Fill a medium saucepan approximately one-third full of oil and heat over medium heat until it reaches 170°C (340°F). If you don't have a thermometer, check the temperature by inserting the end of a wooden spoon or chopstick into the oil. If the oil is hot enough, the wood should sizzle. Note that deep-frying without a thermometer will require some trial and error. If you find that the doughnuts are browning too quickly without cooking all the way through, turn the heat down. Alternatively, if your doughnuts are taking too long to brown, resulting in an oily cooked doughnut, increase the heat slightly and wait for the oil temperature to rise.

11. When the doughnuts have proved for 35 minutes, start cooking them in the hot oil, being careful not to overcrowd the saucepan. When the doughnuts are golden brown on one side (this should take 1–1.5 minutes), turn them over. You may need to turn them over two or three times to ensure they brown evenly.

12. When ready, the doughnuts should have puffed up and will be a rich golden brown. Remove them from the oil and place on a draining rack. Allow to cool for about 2–3 minutes, then dunk in the cinnamon sugar coating if using. Once coated, place the doughnut on a clean rack to cool completely.

13. If filling with jam, custard or salted caramel, use a small serrated knife to pierce the doughnut from one side. Wiggle the knife gently from side to side inside the doughnut to expand the space for filling

14. Fill the doughnuts with your desired filling using a piping bag, then serve immediately.

Jam filling

250 g (9 oz) frozen strawberries
30 g (1 oz) caster (superfine) sugar
10 ml (¼ fl oz) lemon juice

1. Heat the strawberries in a medium saucepan over medium-low heat. As they start to thaw, add the sugar and lemon juice and continue to heat, stirring occasionally as the berries thaw completely.

2. Continue to cook over low heat for 15–20 minutes, stirring occasionally to help the berries break down.

3. When the berries reach a jam-like consistency, remove from the heat and allow to cool (it will continue to thicken as it cools).

4. Blitz with a stick blender or in a food processor, then place in a piping bag to fill the prepared doughnuts.

Custard filling

3 egg yolks
2 tbsp caster (superfine) sugar
2 tbsp GF cornstarch
185 ml (6 fl oz) milk
125 ml (4 fl oz) single cream
⅛ tsp salt
1 tsp vanilla bean paste (or extract)

1. Combine the egg yolks, sugar and cornstarch in a medium bowl and whisk until pale and creamy.

2. Heat the milk, cream, salt and vanilla in a medium saucepan until just simmering, stirring consistently with a spatula to prevent the liquid catching on the base of the pan.

3. Slowly pour the hot milk into the egg yolk mixture, whisking briskly and constantly until fully combined.

4. Transfer the mixture to a clean saucepan and heat again over low heat, whisking constantly until it thickens into a thick custard.

5. Transfer to a clean bowl and cover with plastic wrap, ensuring that the plastic is directly in contact with the surface of the custard (this prevents a skin forming). Set aside to cool.

6. Once cooled, whisk the custard to ensure it is smooth, transfer to a piping bag and fill the prepared doughnuts.

Salted caramel filling

120 g (4 ½ oz) caster (superfine) sugar
30 ml (1 fl oz) water
65 ml (2 ¼ fl oz) single cream
15 g (½ oz) butter
½ tsp salt flakes

1. Weigh the sugar into a medium saucepan and add the water, agitating gently until all the sugar has been moistened.

2. Place over medium heat, bring to the boil and allow the mixture to simmer without touching it for 6–7 minutes. It will come to a rapid boil and start to thicken.

3. Meanwhile, pour the cream into a microwave-safe jug and heat for 30–45 seconds.

4. As the color of the sugar starts to change, keep a very close eye on it as it can burn very rapidly. Reduce the heat to low and wait until it becomes a rich amber color.

5. Quickly remove from the heat and add the hot cream. Be careful as it will bubble vigorously and release a lot of very hot steam. As soon as possible, whisk to combine the caramel with the cream. If it is not coming together, place back over low heat and whisk until combined.

6. Remove from the heat and whisk in the butter. Add the salt, then pour into a clean bowl to cool.

7. Once cooled, transfer the caramel to a piping bag and fill the prepared doughnuts.

Pastries, Cakes and Tarts

Baking gluten-free sweets is probably where I first got my foot in the door of the GF cooking game. Contrary to what people might think, desserts are some of the easiest recipes to convert because most cakes, tarts, and pastries don't rely on gluten for texture. Instead, the focus might be on incorporating eggs in a specific way, or mixing the sugar and butter correctly.

Hopefully this means that the recipes in this section might be a little more familiar if you're just stepping into gluten-free cooking and could be a great place to start. Some of the recipes (like a few of the tarts) are a little technical or appear complex in that there are multiple elements, but don't let that put you off. None of those elements are especially difficult but rather just a little time-consuming.

Choux Pastry

This is a delicate French pastry that forms a nicely hollow shell, perfect to fill with any number of delectable creamy fillings. Choux is probably most recognizable in the form of profiteroles or éclairs, but it is also the backbone of choux au craquelin, the crispy cousin of the profiterole, and the Paris–Brest. As choux is the building block for a number of the pastries to follow in this book, I've kept the recipe for the dough separate below. Use this recipe alongside the one specific to each individual baked goodie.

A note on my choux pastry: I use a slightly unorthodox method of combining the eggs into the dough. Most recipes require you to cool the dough prior to adding the eggs, but I find that GF dough solidifies too much as it cools, making it very difficult to create a smooth pastry when you add the eggs later. As such, I recommend mixing the eggs in straight away (but very slowly), whisking at a high speed so as not to scramble them by allowing prolonged contact with the hot dough. Unfortunately, this makes mixing without electric beaters or a stand mixer very difficult.

250 ml (8½ fl oz) water
110 g (4 oz) butter
¼ tsp salt
200 g (7 oz) whole eggs (about 4 large eggs)
125 g (4½ oz) rice flour

1. Add the water, butter and salt to a medium saucepan over medium heat. As you wait for that to come to a simmer, weigh out the eggs into a jug and whisk until homogenous. Set aside.

2. When the water has come to a boil and the butter has melted, reduce the temperature to low and add the rice flour, quickly mixing with a spatula or wooden spoon to bring the dough together.

3. Continue to mix the dough over low heat for approximately 20 seconds before removing the saucepan from the heat.

4. Transfer the dough to a large bowl (or the bowl of a stand mixer fitted with the whisk attachment) and start beating on medium-high speed.

5. Slowly trickle the eggs into the bowl while continuing to beat at medium-high speed. At no point should the egg puddle in the mixer bowl, so you may need to stop trickling in the eggs briefly to allow the dough to combine.

6. When all the eggs are incorporated into the dough, increase the speed of the stand mixer to high and beat for 3–4 minutes. The dough should be dense but smooth and pipeable.

7. Piping directions and cooking times vary, so when the dough is ready, refer back to the recipe specific to the item being made.

Profiteroles

Makes about 24

NUT FREE   SOY FREE   VEGETARIAN

Profiteroles are probably the simplest version of choux pastry you can make, so they're a great starting point if you haven't made this kind of pastry before. Don't be too concerned if your profiteroles turn out a little wonky – that just means that the blobs of choux you piped weren't uniform. But they'll still be delicious! The filling for these is very simple to keep this recipe beginner-friendly, but feel free to mix it up and fill with your favorite flavored cream or custard.

1 portion of Choux Pastry (page 150)

Filling
600 ml (20 ½ fl oz) whipping or double cream
50 g (1 ¾ oz) GF icing sugar
1 tsp vanilla bean paste (or extract)

Chocolate topping
50 g (1 ¾ oz) dark chocolate, chopped
10 g (¼ oz) butter
1 tbsp single cream

1. Line a large baking tray with parchment paper and preheat your oven to 190°C (375°F).

2. Prepare the Choux Pastry according to the instructions on page 150. Transfer the dough to a piping bag fitted with a round nozzle approximately 1–1.5 cm (½ in) wide.

3. Pipe small blobs about the size of a golf ball onto the prepared baking tray, ensuring you leave 3–4 cm (about 1 ½ in) between each one.

4. Once all the pastry has been piped, wet the tip of your finger and prod down any sharp points or irregularities in the blobs as these will burn and affect the uniformity of your profiteroles.

5. Place the tray in the middle of your oven and bake for 30–35 minutes. The profiteroles should have puffed to two or three times their original size and be golden in color.

6. Open the oven door and, working quickly, use a skewer or small, sharp knife to pierce the base of each profiterole. Leave them upside down on the tray and close the oven door, allowing them to bake for a further 10–15 minutes.

7. Turn the oven off and open the door only slightly to avoid a sudden drop in temperature. Leave for 15 minutes.

8. Remove the profiteroles from the oven, transfer to a cooling rack, and allow to cool completely while you make the filling.

9. Pour the cream into a large mixing bowl and sift in the icing sugar. Add the vanilla and whisk with an electric whisk or beaters until stiff peaks form. Cover and set aside in the fridge.

→

10. To prepare the profiteroles to be filled, use either a sharp paring knife to cut a small cross in the base of each one or puncture the bases with the short end of a round piping tip to create a small, round hole. Alternatively, the profiteroles can be cut in half horizontally, allowing the cream to be piped directly inside (if following this method, proceed first to the next step of making the glaze as dipping the tops of the profiteroles in chocolate should be done prior to filling).

11. When the profiteroles have cooled completely, make the chocolate glaze by combining the chopped chocolate, butter and cream in a heatproof bowl.

12. Melt the ingredients together using a double boiler or by microwaving in 30-second increments. When the glaze ingredients have melted, mix well to combine into a smooth, runny chocolate mixture.

13. To finish the profiteroles, transfer the whipped cream to a piping bag fitted with a small, round piping tip. Fill them with the cream through the holes created in the base.

14. Once filled, hold the profiteroles at the base and dip the tops into the glaze. You may need to use a spoon or spatula to spread the coating a little. If the glaze thickens too much to dip as it cools, reheat it slightly and stir again.

15. Serve immediately or store in an airtight container in the fridge for two or three days. Note that the profiteroles will soften after prolonged contact with the cream, so they will lose their crisp texture if not consumed quickly, but they will still taste good.

Caramel Paris-Brests

Makes 6–8

These pretty pastries are actually supposed to represent the wheel of a bike, having been designed in celebration of a bike race from Paris to Brest, a town in Brittany, France. I actually never got to try one of these decadent desserts before my celiac diagnosis, meaning that they were at the top of my agenda once I'd perfected GF choux pastry.

This recipe, along with my Pistachio Paris-Brests (page 159), is reasonably complex, but the end result is so delicious! These will be best tackled by someone feeling like taking on a bit of a challenge. The good news is that all the elements for this dessert can be made ahead of time (note that the caramel ganache needs 6–8 hours to set before assembling). Just keep the components in separate airtight containers in the fridge (the caramel will need to be reheated slightly before use).

1 portion of Choux Pastry (page 150)
GF icing sugar, to dust
hazelnuts or peanuts, to garnish (optional)

Caramel ganache

4 tsp water
10 g (¼ oz) powdered gelatine
200 g (7 oz) white chocolate, chopped
170 g (6 oz) caster (superfine) sugar
460 ml (15 ½ fl oz) whipping or double cream

Craquelin

45 g (1 ½ oz) butter
50 g (1 ¾ oz) soft brown sugar
50 g (1 ¾ oz) Basic Plain Flour Blend (page 11)

Salted caramel

120 g (4 ½ oz) caster (superfine) sugar
30 ml (1 fl oz) water
65 ml (2 ¼ fl oz) single cream
15 g (½ oz) butter
½ tsp salt flakes

Caramel ganache

1. Start by making the caramel ganache in advance as this needs to set for 6–8 hours. Add the water to a small bowl or jug, then sprinkle the powdered gelatine over the water. Don't stir, just set aside.

2. Place the chopped white chocolate into a deep bowl and set aside. Place the sugar into a medium saucepan, shaking it gently to evenly distribute the sugar over the base of the pan and place over medium heat. Do not stir yet.

3. The edges of the sugar will melt and start to turn amber in color. Gently shake the pan to distribute some of the unmelted sugar into the caramel. Heat the cream in the microwave for about a minute or use a separate saucepan.

4. When about half of the sugar has caramelized, use a wooden spoon or spatula to stir the remaining sugar granules through the caramel. Watch carefully to make sure it doesn't burn. If there are large chunks of solid sugar, lower the heat to allow them to melt. When the sugar mixture has reached a golden caramel color, remove from the heat and carefully add the hot cream and whisk to combine. Be very careful as this will bubble and release a lot of steam.

→

5. When the caramel is smooth, set it aside for a moment. The gelatine mixture should resemble a thick gel with no dry powder visible. Scoop this into the bowl with the chocolate, then pour the hot caramel over the gelatine and chocolate. Let sit for about a minute, then use a stick blender to blitz the mixture into a smooth ganache. Alternatively, whisk or stir the mixture very well and pass through a sieve to remove any inconsistencies.

6. Transfer the ganache to a clean bowl or container and cover with plastic wrap, ensuring that the plastic is directly in contact with all of the exposed ganache (this prevents a skin forming on the surface). Place it in the fridge to set for 6–8 hours.

Craquelin

1. When the ganache has set, begin to make the Paris–Brests starting with the craquelin, which is the crunchy topping that will bake on top of the Choux Pastry. Cream the butter and sugar together using an electric mixer until light and fluffy. Add the flour and combine to create a dough.

2. Transfer the dough to a large sheet of baking paper (about 40 cm or 16 in long) and place a second sheet of the same size on top. Flatten the dough into a rough disc using your hands, then use a rolling pin to smooth the dough out into a thin layer 3–4 mm (about ⅛ in) thick sandwiched between the baking sheets. Transfer the craquelin (still sandwiched between the baking paper) onto a large flat baking tray or chopping board and place it in the freezer. Keep it as flat as possible.

Choux pastry

1. While the craquelin chills, line a large baking tray with parchment paper and preheat your oven to 190°C (375°F), then prepare the Choux Pastry according to the instructions on page 150.

2. Transfer the dough to a piping bag fitted with a large round nozzle approximately 2 cm (¾ in) wide. Pipe the dough onto the prepared baking tray in large, evenly shaped rings, about 12 cm (4¾ in) in diameter. Be sure to space them 6–7 cm (2½ in) apart. You may need a second baking tray.

3. Once the choux has been piped, set the trays aside and take the craquelin out of the freezer. Select two cookie cutters, one slightly larger than the rings of pastry you have piped and one slightly smaller than the hole in the centre of the piped pastry. Use these to cut doughnut-shaped pieces out of the craquelin and place them directly on top of the choux, lining them up as neatly as possible. If you don't have appropriately sized cookie cutters, you can cut the circles of craquelin using a small bowl or plate as a guide.

4. When all the choux has been topped with craquelin, place the trays in the oven and bake for 30–32 minutes. When the pastries are cooked, turn the oven off and open the door a crack. Leave the choux in the oven for a further 10–15 minutes.

5. Remove the pastries and use a butter knife or pallet knife to trim away any craquelin that has pooled at the base of the Paris–Brests. This should scrape away easily while they are still hot but will need to be snapped off when cooled, so work reasonably quickly. Set them aside to cool completely while you make the caramel.

Salted caramel

1. Place the sugar and water into a medium saucepan over medium-low heat. Stir it gently just to ensure that the sugar is all wettened. Allow it to simmer untouched for 4–5 minutes. It will come to a rapid boil and start to thicken.

2. Heat the cream in the microwave for 30–45 seconds (or use a separate saucepan).

3. When the sugar mixture has reached a golden, caramel color, remove from the heat and carefully add the hot cream, whisking to combine. Be very careful as this will bubble and release a lot of steam. When the cream has been fully incorporated, add the butter and whisk until melted, then season with the salt flakes and set aside to cool.

Assembly

1. When the Paris–Brests have cooled completely, transfer the caramel ganache to a large mixing bowl or the bowl of a stand mixer. Begin whisking on low speed for 15–20 seconds, then increase to medium-high speed. Whisk until the ganache thickens, expands in volume and holds stiff peaks. Transfer to a piping bag fitted with an open star nozzle (or other piping tip of your choice).

2. Use a small, sharp knife to cut the Paris–Brests horizontally through the middle. Use your fingers to scrape or pull out any excess choux that hasn't crisped while cooking.

3. Transfer the cooled salted caramel to a piping bag and cut 0.5–1 cm (¼–½ in) off the tip. Drizzle a small amount of caramel into the base of each Paris–Brest.

4. Next, pipe a generous amount of the whipped caramel ganache into the base of each one before gently replacing all the tops.

5. Dust the Paris–Brests with icing sugar. If desired, pipe another small stream of caramel on top and use nuts to garnish. Serve fresh or store in an airtight container in the fridge.

Pistachio Paris-Brests

Makes 6–8

Just like the Caramel Paris–Brests recipe (page 155), these are slightly challenging but utterly luxurious and delicious. The pistachio ganache (made 6–8 hours in advance) is rich and silky, making for the perfect complement to the crunchy choux pastry. Note that pistachio butter can be purchased in jars like peanut butter. It has a thick and creamy paste-like consistency with a very decadent flavor that's a little like white chocolate. You can usually find it in specialty food shops or online. I'm yet to come across one that isn't gluten-free, but still be sure to check the label, just to be safe.

1 portion of Choux Pastry (page 150)
GF icing sugar, to dust
pistachio butter, extra to garnish (optional)
shelled raw pistachios (unsalted), to garnish
   (optional)

Pistachio ganache

1 tbsp water
6 g (1 ¾ tsp) powdered gelatine
200 g (7 oz) white chocolate, chopped
40 g (1 ½ oz) glucose syrup
500 ml (17 fl oz) whipping or double cream
130 g (4 ½ oz) pistachio butter
⅛ tsp salt

Craquelin

45 g (1 ½ oz) shelled raw pistachios (unsalted)
45 g (1 ½ oz) butter
50 g (1 ¾ oz) caster (superfine) sugar
15 g (½ oz) Basic Plain Flour Blend (page 11)

Pistachio ganache

1. Start by making the pistachio ganache in advance as this needs to set for 6–8 hours. Measure the water into a small bowl or jug, then sprinkle the powdered gelatine over the water. Don't stir, just set aside.

2. Place the chopped white chocolate and glucose into a deep bowl and set aside.

3. Place the cream, pistachio butter and salt in a medium pan and place it over medium-low heat, stirring regularly with a spatula.

4. When the gelatine mixture resembles a thick gel with no dry powder visible, scoop this into the bowl with the chocolate and glucose. Just as the cream starts to simmer, pour it over the chocolate, glucose and gelatine. Let it sit for about a minute, then use a stick blender to blitz the mixture into a smooth ganache. Alternatively, whisk or stir the mixture very well and pass through a sieve to remove any inconsistencies.

5. Transfer the ganache to a clean bowl or container and cover with plastic wrap, ensuring that the plastic is directly in contact with all of the exposed ganache (this prevents a skin forming on the surface). Place it in the fridge to set for 6–8 hours.

→

Craquelin

1. When the ganache has set, begin to make the Paris–Brests starting with the craquelin, which is the crunchy topping that will bake on top of the choux. Place the pistachios in a food processor or blender and blitz them to a coarse powder.

2. In a large mixing bowl, cream the butter and sugar together using an electric mixer until light and fluffy. Add the flour and ground pistachios and combine to create a dough.

3. Transfer the dough to a large sheet of baking paper (about 40 cm or 16 in long) and place a second sheet of the same size on top. Flatten the dough into a rough disc using your hands, then use a rolling pin to smooth the dough out into a thin layer 3–4 mm (about ⅛ in) thick sandwiched between the baking sheets. Transfer it (still sandwiched by the baking paper) onto a large flat baking tray or chopping board and place it in the freezer. Keep it as flat as possible.

Choux pastry

1. While the craquelin chills, line a large baking tray with parchment paper and preheat your oven to 190°C (375°F), then prepare the Choux Pastry according to the instructions on page 150. Transfer the dough to a piping bag fitted with a large round nozzle approximately 2 cm (¾ in) wide.

2. Pipe the dough onto the prepared baking tray in large, evenly shaped rings about 12 cm (4¾ in) in diameter. Be sure to space them 6–7 cm (2½ in) apart. You may need a second baking tray.

3. Once the choux has been piped, set the trays aside and take the craquelin out of the freezer. Select two cookie cutters, one slightly large than the rings of pastry you have piped and one slightly smaller than the hole in the centre of the piped pastry. Use these to cut doughnut-shaped pieces out of the craquelin and place them directly on top of the choux, lining them up as neatly as possible. If you don't have appropriately sized cookie cutters, you can cut the circles of craquelin using a small bowl or plate as a guide.

4. When all the choux has been topped with craquelin, place the trays in the oven and bake for 30–32 minutes. When the pastries are cooked, turn the oven off and open the door a crack. Leave the choux in the oven for a further 10–15 minutes.

5. Remove the pastries and use a butter knife or pallet knife to trim away any craquelin that has pooled at the base of the Paris–Brests. This should scrape away easily while they are still hot but will need to be snapped off when cooled, so work reasonably quickly. Set them aside to cool completely.

Assembly

1. When the Paris–Brests have cooled completely, transfer the pistachio ganache to a large mixing bowl or the bowl of a stand mixer. Begin whisking on low speed for 15–20 seconds, then increase to medium-high speed. Whisk until the ganache thickens, expands in volume and holds stiff peaks. Transfer to a piping bag fitted with an open star nozzle (or other piping tip of your choice).

2. Use a small, sharp knife to cut the Paris–Brests horizontally through the middle. Use your fingers to scrape or pull out any excess choux that hasn't crisped while cooking.

3. Pipe a generous amount of the whipped ganache into the base of each one before gently replacing all the tops.

4. Dust the Paris–Brests with icing sugar. If desired, drizzle with a little extra pistachio paste and top with pistachios to garnish. Serve fresh or store in an airtight container in the fridge.

Chocolate Éclairs

Makes 6–8

NUT FREE   SOY FREE   VEGETARIAN

Éclairs are another popular iteration of choux pastry, slightly more difficult than profiteroles due to the piping style, but easier than Paris–Brests. These are particularly decadent as I opted to fill them with a rich and luxurious chocolate custard.

1 portion of Choux Pastry (page 150)

Chocolate crème patissiere

200 g (7 oz) dark chocolate, chopped
3 egg yolks
2 tbsp caster (superfine) sugar
1 ½ tbsp GF cornstarch
150 ml (5 fl oz) milk
150 ml (5 fl oz) single cream
⅛ tsp salt

Chocolate glaze

50 g (1 ¾ oz) dark chocolate, chopped
10 g (¼ oz) butter
1 tbsp single cream

Chocolate crème patissiere

1. Start by making the chocolate crème patissiere filling as this needs to cool before filling the pastries. Place the chopped dark chocolate into a large mixing bowl and set aside.

2. Combine the egg yolks, sugar and cornstarch in a medium bowl and whisk until pale and creamy.

3. Heat the milk, cream and salt in a medium saucepan until just simmering, stirring consistently with a spatula to prevent the liquid catching on the base of the pan.

4. Slowly pour the hot milk into the egg yolk mixture, whisking briskly and constantly until fully combined. Transfer to a clean saucepan and warm again over low heat, whisking constantly until a very thick and creamy custard has formed.

5. Pour it into the bowl with the chocolate. Allow to sit for about a minute, then whisk well until the chocolate has melted and is fully incorporated into the custard.

6. Cover with plastic wrap, ensuring that the plastic is directly in contact with the surface of the custard (this prevents a skin forming). Place in the fridge to cool while you make the choux pastry.

→

Choux pastry

1. Line a large baking tray with parchment paper and preheat your oven to 190°C (375°F), then prepare the Choux Pastry according to the instructions on page 150. Transfer the dough to a piping bag fitted with an open star tip approximately 1.5 cm (½ in) wide. Pipe straight 9–10 cm (3½–4 in) logs onto the prepared baking tray, ensuring you leave 3–4 cm (1½ in) between each one.

2. Once all the pastry has been piped, wet the tip of your finger and prod down or smooth any large lumps or irregularities in piping as these will affect the uniformity of your éclairs.

3. Place the tray in the middle of your oven and bake for 30–35 minutes. The éclairs should have puffed to at least twice their original size and be golden in color.

4. Open the oven door and, working quickly, use a skewer or small, sharp knife to pierce the base of each éclair in three places along the length. Leave them upside down on the tray and close the oven door, allowing them to bake for a further 10–15 minutes.

5. Turn the oven off and open the door only slightly to avoid a sudden drop in temperature. Leave for 15 minutes.

6. Remove the éclairs from the oven, transfer to a cooling rack and allow to cool completely.

7. To prepare the éclairs to be filled, use either a sharp paring knife to cut small crosses in the base of each one (over the small holes you created earlier) or just widen the small punctures you already made using the short end of a round piping tip. Alternatively, the éclairs can be cut in half horizontally, allowing the filling to be piped directly inside (if following this method, proceed first to the next step of making the glaze as dipping the tops of the éclairs in chocolate should be done prior to filling).

Chocolate glaze

1. When the éclairs have cooled completely, make the chocolate glaze by combining the chopped chocolate, butter and cream in a heatproof bowl.

2. Melt the ingredients together using a double boiler or by microwaving in 30-second increments. When the glaze ingredients have melted, mix well to combine into a smooth, runny chocolate mixture.

Assembly

1. To finish the éclairs, transfer the chocolate crème patissiere to a piping bag fitted with a small round piping tip. Pipe this into the éclairs using the small holes created in the base.

2. Once filled, dip the éclairs into the glaze, just deep enough to cover the top of each one. Neaten the chocolate glaze with your finger or a small spatula, then place carefully onto a cooling rack to set.

3. Serve immediately or store in an airtight container in the fridge for two or three days. Note that the éclairs will soften after prolonged contact with the filling, so they will lose their crisp texture if not consumed quickly, but will continue to taste good!

Filo Pastry

Makes 1 portion

This is one of the recipes I'm most proud to include in my book. It has taken a *lot* of trial and error, heaps of time and enormous amounts of research to create a pastry that can be rolled thin enough for baklava, spanakopita and other famous filo-based recipes.

A note regarding this recipe: egg white powder is an ingredient found in specialty stores or online. It is not absolutely *essential* for this recipe – the filo can be made without it – however, the egg white provides a protein source that contributes to the elasticity and structural integrity of the pastry. As such, it will be harder (but not impossible) to roll the pastry as thin as you can when it is included. You will find that the end product is a little more brittle and difficult to work with, and it is more likely to tear or develop small holes as you roll it by hand. Even so, as filo recipes generally call for multiple overlapping layers, small holes are not hugely problematic, so if you can't find egg white powder, don't be discouraged.

180 g (6½ oz) Basic Plain Flour Blend (page 11)
3 tsp psyllium husk powder
2 tsp xanthan gum
2 tsp caster (superfine) sugar
1 tsp egg white powder
¼ tsp salt
135 ml (4½ fl oz) very warm water
25 g (1 oz) butter, melted

1. Sift together the dry ingredients in the bowl of your stand mixer (or other large bowl) and create a well in the centre.

2. Add the wet ingredients and combine using a paddle attachment on a stand mixer at medium-low speed or a sturdy spatula. Once the dough has come together, continue mixing vigorously (medium speed in stand mixer for 5–6 minutes, or for about 10 minutes by hand). The dough should be soft, warm and pliable.

3. Divide the dough into four equal pieces and place these in a ziplock bag or airtight container so they don't dry out as you roll them out one at a time.

4. The easiest way to roll out the dough balls is with a mechanical pasta roller, but they can also be rolled with a rolling pin. Each ball will be rolled into a sheet less than 0.5 mm thick. If using a pasta roller, use a rolling pin to roll the dough out to be approximately 1 cm (½ in) thick, then start using the pasta roller on the widest setting.

5. Pass the dough through the roller once, fold the dough over on itself in three portions (like you might fold a letter), then rotate and feed it through the machine again. You might need to use a rolling pin to assist in getting it thin enough after the fold.

→

6. Feed the dough repeatedly through the pasta roller, changing to a narrower setting each time it passes through. To get even edges along the dough, periodically fold the dough into a rectangle as close to the width of the roller as possible, increase to a wider setting on the pasta roller and feed it through again. You may also need to dust the dough lightly with flour if it is sticking to the roller.

7. When you have rolled it to the narrowest setting on the machine or have rolled it out by hand (the sheet of dough will be roughly 100 cm or 40 in) in length), flour your work surface and lay out the filo. Dust it well with flour, then cut it in half to form two sheets of a more workable length (they should both be approximately 14 x 50 cm or 6 x 20 in). Set one aside.

8. Starting from the centre of the sheet, use a rolling pin to roll outwards. Do this in all directions, concentrating on rolling the dough from the centre to the outer edges. Make sure to lift and move the dough as you work, dusting it and the work surface with flour as necessary to prevent it from sticking. The dough should be pliable and be able to stretch slightly, but it will tear easily if an edge catches on the rolling pin.

9. When the dough is about 0.2–0.3 mm thick (it should feel similar to a cotton bedsheet), fold it up gently (ensuring it has been dusted with enough flour to prevent sticking) and either wrap it in plastic or place it in an airtight container.

10. Repeat with the other half of the rolled sheet, then repeat the rolling process with the remaining dough balls. This will yield eight sheets measuring approximately 22 x 55 cm (9 x 22 in).

11. The filo can be used straight away or will keep in the fridge for two or three days if wrapped well in plastic. Simply unroll the sheets of filo and use a pastry brush to brush off excess flour before use.

Baklava

Serves 6–8

This is honestly one of the holy grails of gluten-free cooking, and even having made it more than half a dozen times, it still blows me away every time. I never thought I'd achieve the thinness of filo, and then even when I did, there was no guarantee that it would bake evenly through the many flaky layers ... but it does! In this recipe I've kept the sugar syrup and nut mixture incredibly simple because there are so many variations of baklava out there. Feel free to adjust it to your tastes or your own family traditions, because the real magic here is the filo, and it goes well with everything.

1 portion of Filo Pastry (page 167)
180 g (6 ½ oz) shelled raw pistachios (unsalted)
45 g (1 ½ oz) ghee, melted
300 g (10 ½ oz) caster (superfine) sugar
180 ml (6 fl oz) water
10–12 cardamom pods

1. Make the Filo Pastry according to the directions on page 167. Once the sheets have been rolled according to those instructions (yielding eight sheets approximately 22 x 55 cm or 9 x 22 in), cut them in half again to fit into a deep stainless steel baking dish about 26 x 20 cm or 10 x 8 in (ceramic or glass oven-safe dishes are not recommended as they may crack later when the cool syrup is poured over the hot baklava). You should now have sixteen sheets approximately the size of the baking tray. Set the pastry aside.

2. Preheat the oven to 180°C (360°F).

3. Weigh the nuts into the canister of a food processor and blitz until they resemble breadcrumbs. Remove 30 g (1 oz) and set aside for garnishing later.

4. To start assembling the baklava, use a dry pastry brush to remove any excess flour from the filo sheets. Lay the first sheet into the baking dish and spread a light layer of ghee over the surface with a pastry brush.

5. Lay the second sheet on top of the first and brush on another layer of ghee. Repeat until you have eight layers of pastry in the tray. Don't brush the top layer with ghee.

6. Take the pistachios remaining in the food processor and sprinkle them all over the surface in a generous, even layer, then repeat the layering process with eight more sheets of ghee-brushed filo. Brush the top sheet with ghee.

7. Use a sharp knife to cut the baklava in straight, even lines down the length of the baking tray. Then rotate the tray 45 degrees and repeat the straight, even cuts. This will create a diamond pattern over the baklava.

8. Cover the tray in aluminium foil then bake for 50 minutes. While waiting, make the sugar syrup.

9. Weigh the caster sugar into a medium saucepan. Add the water and cardamom pods. Place on high heat until it comes to a boil, then reduce the heat to medium and let simmer for 10–12 minutes. Remove from the heat and allow to cool.

10. When the baklava has baked for 50 minutes, remove the aluminium foil and bake for a further 12–14 minutes or until the pastry is crisp and evenly cooked.

11. Remove the tray from the oven and place it on a cooling rack. Remove the cardamom pods from the syrup and carefully drizzle it over the baklava. Go slowly as it will bubble when it hits the hot oven tray and may overflow if the tray isn't deep enough.

12. Garnish with the pistachios set aside earlier and allow to cool before serving.

Vanilla Party Cake with Swiss Meringue Buttercream

Serves 6–8

This is called a party cake because it's the *perfect* cake to make for any event where you want a gluten-free option but don't want people to be able to guess that it's not a 'normal' cake. It's light and airy but has enough structural integrity to be made into a stable layer cake, so it's great for birthdays. I even made a two-tier version (doubling the recipe) for a larger event and was asked to make it for someone's wedding … and they weren't even GF! If you're looking to make it a little more exciting, try adding a tablespoon or two of lemon zest with the sugar to make this into a really lovely lemon cake (just omit or use less vanilla).

180 g (6½ oz) butter, softened
180 g (6½ oz) caster (superfine) sugar
1½ tsp vanilla bean paste (or extract)
3 eggs
180 g (6½ oz) Basic Plain Flour Blend (page 11)
1½ tsp GF baking powder
⅓ tsp salt
85 ml (2¾ fl oz) milk, at room temperature
jam or curd for filling (optional — see doughnut fillings
     pages 146–147)

Swiss meringue buttercream

4 egg whites (about 145 g or 5 oz)
145 g (5 oz) caster (superfine) sugar
⅛ tsp cream of tartar
260 g (9 oz) cubed butter, at room temperature
⅛ tsp salt
2 tsp vanilla bean paste (or extract)

1. Preheat oven to 160°C (320°F) and grease and line two round 14 cm (5½ in) cake tins.

2. In a large mixing bowl or the bowl of a stand mixer fitted with a whisk attachment, cream together the butter, sugar and vanilla.

3. Add the eggs one at a time, beating constantly until the mixture is light and fluffy.

4. In a separate bowl, sift together the flour, baking powder and salt.

5. Fold in the milk and dry ingredients by hand, mixing until just incorporated and smooth.

6. Divide the batter between the two cake tins and even out the surface with a spatula or palette knife. Bake for 35–40 minutes or until a skewer inserted into the centre of the cakes comes out clean. Allow them to cool in the tins for 10–15 minutes before turning them out onto a cooling rack.

7. While waiting for the cakes to cool completely, make the Swiss meringue buttercream. Start by preparing a double boiler.

8. Place the egg whites, sugar and cream of tartar in a large bowl or the bowl of your stand mixer. Whisk briefly with a handheld whisk to combine. Place the bowl over the heat and whisk constantly until the sugar has dissolved and the temperature of the egg whites reaches 60°C (140°F).

→

9. Remove the bowl from the heat and start whisking with an electric whisk, beater or a stand mixer fitted with a whisk attachment. Start on low to medium speed for about a minute, then increase to high speed.

10. Whisk until stiff peaks form (this can take 10–15 minutes, depending on your mixer), then start adding the butter piece by piece while continuing to whisk on high speed. Initially, the meringue will fall and lose its volume. Continue adding pieces of butter. The meringue will start to look as though it is curdling or separating. This is normal – continue whisking on high speed, gradually adding butter.

11. The mixture will eventually come back together as the butter emulsifies with the egg whites – this may take another 10–15 minutes. When the buttercream is homogenous, light and fluffy, add the salt and vanilla.

12. Switch to the paddle attachment and beat at medium speed for a further 6–8 minutes to remove some of the air bubbles in the icing (this will make icing the cake easier). If you aren't using a stand mixer with a paddle attachment, mix the icing by hand with a large spatula to manually remove the air bubbles instead. Color the icing however you'd like, then set aside until you assemble the cake.

13. When the cakes have cooled completely, trim the domed tops (these can be snacked on or reserved for cakepops), then cut the cakes in half horizontally to create four flat layers. Use the bottom half of each cake as the bottom and top layers of the final cake as these will have the most uniform surface.

14. Place a small amount of buttercream in the centre of a cakeboard or serving plate, then place one of the cake bottoms (cut side up) on top of the buttercream and apply some pressure, sticking it into place.

15. Dollop 4–5 tbsp of the buttercream onto the cake and smooth it out into an even layer with a palette knife or spatula. If filling the cake with jam or curd, add an extra 2–3 tbsp of icing, but then scoop out some of the icing from the centre of this layer of buttercream, leaving a solid wall of icing remaining around the edge of the cake. Fill this cavity with jam or curd before stacking the next cake layer on top.

16. Place the next layer of cake on top and repeat the process with the buttercream (and filling if desired). Repeat with the third cake layer, ensuring as you go that each layer is lined up perfectly with the one below it.

17. The fourth layer of cake should be the second cake bottom. Place this layer cut side down onto the buttercream on the third cake layer. Press gently into place.

18. Place a large dollop of buttercream on top and smooth it out, pushing the excess icing over the sides of the cake as you go. This is the first of two layers of the buttercream.

19. Smooth the buttercream around the outside of the cake using a cake scraper or offset palette knife, holding it vertically against the side of the cake as you move your hand around its circumference. When this layer is as smooth as possible, place the cake in the fridge for 1–2 hours to allow the buttercream to set. This is known as a 'crumb coat' as it seals any crumbs inside this layer so that you can achieve a very clean look with the second layer of buttercream. This is optional – you can put all the buttercream on at once if you wish.

20. Once the crumb coat has set, use about two-thirds of the remaining buttercream to apply a second layer on the top and sides of the cake, again smoothing and scraping to make it as neat as possible. Any remaining buttercream can be

transferred to a piping bag fitted with a star nozzle and piped on as decoration.

21. When you've achieved the desired look, place the cake in the fridge to set the icing (after which the cake can be wrapped in plastic wrap if necessary), but take out in advance of serving to allow the cake to come to room temperature. Sealing the cake in the buttercream does preserve the freshness of the cake quite well, providing you serve the cake at room temperature. However, if planning to serve the cake more than a day after baking, brush each cake layer liberally with a simple sugar syrup before you layer them (use a 1:1 ratio of caster sugar dissolved in water and flavored with vanilla or lemon juice if desired). This will help to prevent the cake from drying out.

Barbee's Bee Sting Cake

Serves 12–14

This is a decadent cake inspired by the bee sting slices popular in bakeries all over Australia. How close they come to the traditional German version of this sweet I don't know, but I wanted to make a cake reminiscent of those flavors. I will note that this is usually made with a yeast-based dough rather than a cake, but I think this is just as delicious and makes for an interesting change (it also makes it a little simpler). I make mine with honey collected from the beehive on my mum's property, which is affectionately known by my family as Barbee's honey in reference to my mum, Barbara!

250 g (9 oz) sugar
100 g (3 ½ oz) butter
1 tsp vanilla bean paste (or extract)
50 g (1 ¾ oz) honey
6 eggs
210 g (7 ½ oz) Basic Plain Flour Blend (page 11)
2 ½ tsp GF baking powder
½ tsp salt
65 ml (2 ¼ fl oz) milk

Nut brittle topping

100 g (3 ½ oz) honey
40 g (1 ½ oz) sugar
200 g (7 oz) flaked almonds

Honey crème diplomate filling

3 egg yolks
1 tbsp caster (superfine) sugar
30 g (1 oz) honey
2 ½ tbsp GF cornstarch
320 ml (11 fl oz) milk
⅛ tsp salt
500 ml (17 fl oz) whipping or double cream
2 tbsp GF icing sugar
1 tsp vanilla bean paste (or extract)

1. Preheat your oven to 140°C (285°F) and grease and line two 35 x 24 cm (14 x 9 in) cake tins. (If you do not have two cake tins of the same size, split the cake ingredients into two and make the first cake, then bake the nut brittle and assemble the top layer of the cake. Then make the second cake using the same cake tin.)

2. Place the sugar, butter, vanilla and honey in a large bowl and whisk with electric beaters or a stand mixer until light and creamy. Crack the eggs in one at a time, whisking well after each addition.

3. In a separate bowl, sift together the flour, baking powder and salt.

4. Add the flour mixture and milk to the egg mixture in batches, alternating between the dry and the wet, whisking between each addition. You should start and finish with the dry ingredients, so the order of adding the flour and milk should be dry, wet, dry, wet, dry.

5. Divide the batter evenly into the prepared cake tins and bake for 32–35 minutes or until the cake is golden brown and a skewer inserted into the centre of the cakes comes out clean. Allow the cakes to cool in the tins for 5–10 minutes before turning them out onto a cooling rack.

6. To make the nut brittle topping, increase the oven heat to 175°C (350°F) and clean one of the cake tins. Line it again with baking paper.

→

7. Heat the honey and sugar in a medium saucepan until the sugar has dissolved, then add the flaked almonds. Remove from the heat and gently stir the almonds through the honey mixture, ensuring all the nuts are coated while trying not to break up the almond flakes.

8. Pour the almonds into the prepared cake tin and smooth them out into an even layer with a spatula. You can grease your hands with butter and use your fingers to press the nuts into the corners to make it easier, but just be wary of how hot the nuts are.

9. Place the cake tin with the nuts into the oven and bake for 7–8 minutes.

10. Remove the cake tin from the oven and place it on a heatproof surface. Then, working quickly, place one of the honey cakes top side down into the cake tin, directly on top of the nuts. As the nuts cool and harden, they will stick to the top of the cake. Allow to cool in the cake tin for 15–20 minutes before turning out onto a cooling rack.

11. To make the honey crème diplomate filling, whisk the egg yolks, sugar, honey and cornstarch together in a medium bowl.

12. In a saucepan, heat the milk and salt until just simmering, then trickle onto the egg yolk mixture, whisking constantly. When smooth and fully incorporated, tip this honey custard mixture into a clean saucepan and place on medium-low heat.

13. Stir constantly with a spatula until a thick custard has formed, then transfer to a shallow bowl. Cover with plastic wrap so that the plastic touches the surface of the custard to prevent a skin from forming. Set aside to cool.

14. When the custard has cooled completely, use a separate mixing bowl to whisk the cream, icing sugar and vanilla until stiff peaks have formed, then gently fold the cooled custard through the cream until fully combined.

15. To serve the bee sting cake, it is easiest to pre-cut the cake into slices before filling as otherwise the crème diplomate will ooze out when you slice. To do so, lay the cake with the nuts top side down on a large chopping board. Lay the second cake on top and slice into serving sizes.

16. Then, one by one, generously fill each piece with the honey crème diplomate filling before sandwiching the cakes back together.

Lamingtons

Makes 12–14

NUT FREE · SOY FREE · VEGETARIAN

Along with Fingerbuns (page 131), lamingtons are another Aussie classic, and for good reason. They're made from pieces of sponge cake, dipped in chocolate icing, and then covered in coconut. The sponge recipe I use here will ensure that no-one misses out. If you haven't used a double boiler for cakes before, don't let that scare you off – it's really quite simple and creates a beautifully light and airy sponge perfect for single-layer lamington fingers or, if you're feeling adventurous, multi-layer lamingtons sandwiched with strawberry or raspberry jam.

4 eggs (about 200 g or 7 oz)
125 g (4 ½ oz) caster (superfine) sugar
120 g (4 ½ oz) Basic Plain Flour Blend (page 11)
1 ¼ tsp GF baking powder
⅛ tsp salt
1 tsp vanilla bean paste or extract
50 g (1 ¾ oz) butter, melted
250 g (9 oz) desiccated coconut
50 g (1 ¾ oz) shredded coconut (optional)

Icing

60 g (2 oz) dark chocolate, chopped
35 g (1 ¼ oz) butter
500 g (1 lb 2 oz) GF icing sugar
10 g (¼ oz) cocoa powder
130 ml (4 ½ fl oz) boiling water

1. Preheat your oven to 160°C (320°F) and grease and line a 35 x 24 cm (14 x 9 in) baking tray.

2. Prepare a double boiler, then add the eggs and sugar to a large mixing bowl.

3. Place the bowl over the heat, whisking constantly until the sugar has dissolved. This will be about 50°C (120°F) if you have a thermometer, but you can also test by rubbing the mixture between your thumb and forefinger to see if you can feel the sugar granules.

4. Remove the bowl from the heat, then whisk using electric beaters or a stand mixer until it reaches the ribbon stage: this is when you can stop the whisk and, if you lift it out of the bowl, the mixture will stream off it in a thick, glossy ribbon, pooling gently in the bowl. This should take around 4–6 minutes of whisking on high speed.

5. Sift in the flour, baking powder, salt and vanilla, and fold gently with a spatula to combine, removing any lumps while trying to maintain as much air and volume as possible.

6. Add the melted butter and fold again until just combined.

7. Pour the batter into the lined baking tray and smooth to create an even layer. Bake for 20–22 minutes until it is golden on top and a skewer inserted into the sponge comes out clean.

8. Allow to cool in the baking tray for about 10 minutes before removing it, then place it on a rack to cool completely.

9. When the cake has cooled, make the chocolate icing mixture by combining the chocolate and butter in a bowl. Heat in the microwave for 30 seconds at a time, stirring after each interval until the chocolate has melted completely (this can also be done over a double boiler).

10. Sift in the icing sugar and cocoa, then add the boiling water and stir well until no lumps remain. Set aside.

11. Put the desiccated coconut in a bowl and stir through the shredded coconut if using (two types of coconut boosts the coconut flavor and adds a crunch, but this is entirely up to you). Set aside.

12. Slice the sponge into approximately 12 rectangular pieces.

→

13. Set up a work station with the sponge pieces on one side, the bowl of chocolate icing next to them, then the bowl of coconut, then a wire rack placed over a sheet of baking paper to minimize the mess from dripping chocolate.

14. Take a single piece of the sponge and gently place one of the short ends into the bowl of chocolate icing. Using a spoon, pick up the icing and drizzle it over all sides of the sponge. The sponge is very delicate and will break apart if you try to roll it in the chocolate, so use this gentle coating method instead.

15. When the sponge is completely coated in icing, gently remove the excess with the spoon and place the sponge straight into the bowl of coconut.

16. Delicately coat each side with the coconut, then place the sponge on the rack.

17. Repeat with the remaining sponge pieces. The lamingtons are ready to serve straight away and will be best eaten on the day of cooking, but they can also be stored in an airtight container for two or three days.

Hazelnut Meringue Stack

Serves 6–8

It's always useful to have a dessert at hand that is not only tasty when eaten as leftovers but is actually *better* when eaten a day or two after it was made. This is the perfect make-ahead option if you know you're not going to have time to prepare dessert for a dinner with friends or family. The nutty meringue is crisp when first cooked, but once the layers are sandwiched with the crème patissiere and coated in chocolate, they start to soften up in the best way! In saying that, it's definitely delicious eaten fresh as well, but leaving it to soften a little is my favorite way of devouring this ... and it *will* get devoured.

100 g (4 oz) hazelnuts
30 g (1 oz) almond meal
25 g (1 oz) caster (superfine) sugar
10 g (¼ oz) GF cornstarch
3 egg whites
100 g (3 ½ oz) caster (superfine) sugar, extra

Crème patissiere

3 egg yolks
2 tbsp caster (superfine) sugar
2 ½ tbsp GF cornstarch
310 ml (10 ½ fl oz) milk
1 tsp vanilla bean paste or extract
⅛ tsp salt

Chocolate caramel topping

130 g (4 ½ oz) caster (superfine) sugar
200 g (7 oz) milk chocolate, chopped
80 ml (2 ½ fl oz) single cream

1. Preheat oven to 150°C (300°F). Use a plate or bowl to trace three circles approximately 24 cm (9 in) in diameter onto sheets of baking paper. Place the baking paper traced side down onto flat baking trays and set aside.

2. Start by making the meringue layers. Place the hazelnuts, almond meal, caster sugar and cornstarch into a food processor and blitz to a fine crumb. Set aside.

3. Place the egg whites into a large bowl or the bowl of a stand mixer fitted with the whisk attachment. Whisk, starting on low speed before increasing to medium-high.

4. When the egg whites are frothy and voluminous, start adding the extra sugar one tablespoon at a time while continuing to whisk constantly. Whisk until the meringue holds stiff peaks, then fold the blitzed hazelnut mixture gently through the meringue with a spatula. When fully combined, divide the meringue mixture evenly between the baking trays, smoothing the meringue out to fill in the three traced circles so that they are all the same size. Using a piping bag for this step will be easier and help to keep the meringue uniform, but this is optional.

5. Bake the meringues in the oven for 25–30 minutes. They should be lightly brown and crisp to the touch. Set aside to cool completely.

6. To make the crème patissiere, place the egg yolks, sugar and cornstarch in a medium bowl and whisk until pale and creamy.

7. Heat the milk, vanilla and salt in a medium saucepan over medium-low heat, stirring regularly with a spatula.

8. When just simmering, trickle the hot milk into the egg yolk mixture, whisking briskly and constantly until smooth and fully combined. Transfer the mixture into a clean saucepan, place back over medium-low heat and continue whisking until a thick custard has formed (be sure not to let it catch on the base of the saucepan).

9. Transfer to a clean bowl and cover with plastic wrap, ensuring that the plastic is directly in contact with the surface of the custard (this prevents a skin forming). Set aside to cool.

→

10. While waiting for the meringues and crème patissiere to cool, start on the caramel for the topping. This will harden and be crushed into small, crunchy pieces. Prepare a baking tray with a sheet of baking paper.

11. Place the sugar in a clean pan, shaking gently to evenly distribute the sugar over the base and then place over medium heat. Do not stir yet. The edges of the sugar will start to melt and turn amber in color. Gently shake the pan to distribute some of the unmelted sugar into the caramel. When about half of the sugar has caramelized, use a wooden spoon or spatula to stir the remaining sugar granules through the caramel. Watch carefully to make sure it doesn't burn. Lower the heat if there are large chunks of solid sugar.

12. When the sugar is a rich dark caramel color, quickly remove it from the heat and pour onto the baking paper on the prepared tray. Be careful as it will be *very* hot. Gently tilt the baking tray to spread the caramel over the tray into a thin layer. Set aside to cool.

13. When all elements have cooled, begin assembly. Place one meringue disc onto a wire rack and spoon half the crème patissiere into the centre. Use a spatula or palette knife to spread it evenly over the meringue, leaving about 1.5–2 cm (½–¾ in) clear around the rim.

14. Place another layer of meringue on top and repeat the process with the second half of the crème patissiere. Place the third meringue disc on top and push it down gently to make sure all the layers are snugly in place.

15. To finish the topping, start by breaking up the hardened caramel into pieces and placing into a food processor. Pulse until you can see a combination of larger chunks and small crumbs.

16. Combine the chocolate and cream in a microwave-safe bowl. Microwave for 45–60 seconds, then stir well with a spatula to combine the cream and chocolate into a smooth ganache. Tip about three-quarters of the crunchy caramel pieces into the ganache, making sure to keep some of the large chunks separate to garnish.

17. Place the wire rack with the assembled meringue stack onto a baking tray or sheet of baking paper to catch the drippings, then pour some of the chocolate caramel topping onto the stack. Smooth with a spatula or palette knife, then continue pouring the topping to cover the entire cake. Pour in batches to coat it as evenly as possible, spreading it around as necessary. When the cake is entirely covered, top it with the reserved pieces of hardened caramel as desired.

18. To remove the cake from the rack, gently run a knife or palette knife around the base to separate the cake from the ganache caught on the cooling tray, then use a large flat spatula to lift the cake from the base onto a serving plate. The cake will be ready to serve immediately but is best made a day or two beforehand and stored in the fridge so that the meringue softens slightly.

Cheesecake Brownie

Serves 10–12

These are *outrageously* delectable, so while I've indicated that this recipe yields enough for 10 to 12 serves, maybe don't expect it to feed that many people, because everyone will want seconds! I think this takes the best part of a brownie – rich, fudgy, chocolatey goodness – and the best thing about a cheesecake – smooth, creamy decadence – and brings them together to form the ultimate combo of both. It's also deceptively simple and is sure to please everyone.

Cheesecake

250 g (9 oz) cream cheese

70 g (2 ½ oz) caster (superfine) sugar

1 large egg

1 tsp vanilla bean paste

⅛ tsp salt

Brownie

100 g (3 ½ oz) dark chocolate, chopped

100 g (3 ½ oz) milk chocolate, chopped

180 g (6 ½ oz) butter

10 g (¼ oz) cocoa powder

3 large eggs

300 g (10 ½ oz) caster (superfine) sugar

¼ tsp salt

100 g (3 ½ oz) Basic Plain Flour Blend (page 11)

1. Preheat oven to 170°C (340°F) and grease and line a 35 x 24 cm (14 x 9 in) baking tray.

2. Start by making the cheesecake mixture. Place all the cheesecake ingredients into a large bowl and beat with an electric mixer until smooth. Set aside.

3. For the brownie mixture, place the chocolate and butter in a microwave-safe bowl and microwave in 30-second increments until fully melted (you could also use a double boiler). Stir to combine.

4. Sift in the cocoa powder, stir and set aside.

5. In a large bowl, beat eggs, sugar and salt in a stand mixer or with electric beaters until the sugar has dissolved.

6. Add the melted chocolate mixture and whisk briefly to combine.

7. Add the flour and whisk until smooth.

8. Pour the brownie batter into the prepared baking tray, ensuring it is evenly distributed.

9. Place large dollops of the cheesecake mixture onto the brownie batter, then swirl it through with a spoon, butter knife or skewer. Ensure that the cheesecake is distributed so that every slice of brownie will contain some cheesecake.

10. Place in the oven and bake for 25–28 minutes. The brownie will be firm around the edges but quite soft through the middle (this will also firm as it cools but will still be 'fudgy'), and the cheesecake will have browned slightly.

11. Allow to cool in the baking tray for 15–20 minutes before moving it to a rack to cool completely.

12. Cut the brownie into even squares or rectangles (depending on your desired serving size) and store in an airtight container. Keep in the fridge if not being eaten the day of baking.

Ginger Cakes

Makes 10–12

These easy, snack-sized cakes conjure up very nostalgic thoughts of gingerbread and Christmas because of their warm, lightly spiced aroma. Because they're made partially with almond meal, which keeps them perfectly moist, they keep really well in an airtight container for two or three days (especially if you warm them up for a few seconds in the microwave before eating). This recipe also works for muffins, so never mind if you don't have a mini bundt pan.

270 g (9½ oz) soft brown sugar
180 g (6½ oz) butter
3 eggs
120 g (4½ oz) Basic Plain Flour Blend (page 11)
1½ tsp GF baking powder
135 g (5 oz) almond meal
¼ tsp salt
3 tsp ginger powder
2 tsp cinnamon
½ tsp cardamom powder
100 g (3½ oz) milk

Icing
180 g (6½ oz) GF icing sugar
1½ tbsp boiling water
1¼ tsp lemon juice

1. Preheat oven to 170°C (340°F) and grease a mini bundt pan (you can also use a muffin tray).

2. In a large mixing bowl or the bowl of a stand mixer fitted with a whisk attachment, cream the sugar and butter until pale and creamy.

3. Add the eggs and beat well until combined and fluffy.

4. In a separate bowl, sift together the flour, baking powder, almond meal, salt and spices.

5. Add the dry ingredients and milk to the egg mixture in batches, alternating between the dry and the wet, whisking between each addition. You should start and finish with the dry ingredients, so the order of adding the dry ingredients and the milk should be dry, wet, dry, wet, dry.

6. Fill the prepared bundt pans or muffin tray two-thirds full with batter. If using a six-piece bundt pan, you will need to bake in two batches.

7. Bake for 16–18 minutes or until a skewer inserted into the cakes comes out clean.

8. Allow them to cool in the tray for 10–15 minutes before turning them out onto a rack.

9. When the cakes have cooled completely, combine the icing sugar, boiling water and lemon juice in a small bowl. Stir until smooth, then drizzle the icing lightly over the ginger cakes.

10. Serve immediately or store in an airtight container for two or three days.

Brown Butter Banana Bread

Serves 8

Banana bread is a beloved classic for good reason: it's delicious, easy to make and a great use of leftover bananas. I've never wanted to mess with the classic too much but I couldn't resist seeing how brown butter would change my favorite banana bread recipe. It turns out that the slightly caramelized flavor works beautifully with the bananas, and now I would never dream of skipping that step!

100 g (3½ oz) butter

285 g (10 oz) Basic Plain Flour Blend (page 11)

2¾ tsp GF baking powder

230 g (8 oz) caster (superfine) sugar

½ tsp salt

150 g (5½ oz) soft brown sugar

2 large eggs

1 tsp vanilla bean paste or extract

2 large overripe bananas, mashed (about 290 g or 10 oz)

125 ml (4 fl oz) milk

1 banana, extra, to garnish

1. Preheat oven to 160°C (320°F) and grease and line a 28 x 15 cm (11 x 6 in) loaf tin.

2. Start by browning the butter. Place the butter in a saucepan over medium-low heat, stirring occasionally. The butter will foam and slowly change color. When it has stopped foaming, smells slightly nutty and is a golden brown color, remove from the heat and set aside.

3. Sift the dry ingredients together in a large bowl, then form a well in the centre.

4. Add the eggs, vanilla and mashed bananas and begin to mix them, slowly incorporating the flour mixture from the edges of the well.

5. Add the milk and mix all the ingredients until combined.

6. Add the brown butter and stir it through.

7. Pour the batter into the prepared loaf tin and smooth the surface flat.

8. Halve the extra banana lengthwise and place the two halves along the top of the loaf, pressing gently to just submerge them in the batter.

9. Place in the oven and bake for approximately 90 minutes or until a skewer inserted into the centre of the loaf comes out clean (or with just a few moist crumbs attached).

10. Allow to cool in the tin for 15–20 minutes before turning the loaf out onto a wire rack.

11. Serve warm if desired, or allow to cool completely before storing in an airtight container in the fridge.

12. The banana bread is best served warm, at room temperature or toasted lightly in a frying pan.

Souffle Cheesecake

Serves 8

You may not have heard of a souffle cheesecake but you've likely seen videos of these cakes jiggling online. They're quite a light yet moist sponge that carries the delicious cream cheese flavor of a traditional cheesecake without the dense texture. As tempting as it will be, don't eat this cake until it has cooled completely. It is actually most delicious eaten cold out of the fridge as the high egg content can skew the flavor a little if eaten warm. This cake can be made two or three days in advance and stored in the fridge covered or in an airtight container

190 g (6 ½ oz) cream cheese

40 g (1 ½ oz) butter

1 ½ tsp vanilla bean paste

½ tsp salt

4 large eggs, separated (approximately 55 g or 2 oz of yolks and 125 g or 4 ½ oz of whites)

15 g (½ oz) GF cornstarch

25 g (1 oz) Basic Plain Flour Blend (page 11)

95 ml (3 ¼ fl oz) milk

⅛ tsp cream of tartar

110 g (4 oz) caster (superfine) sugar

1. Grease and line a deep, round 18 cm (7 in) cake tin and preheat your oven to 100°C (210°F).

2. Combine the cream cheese, butter, vanilla and salt in a medium saucepan over low heat, stirring constantly until smooth. Remove from the heat and add the egg yolks one at a time, whisking after each addition.

3. Sift in the cornstarch and flour and whisk again until completely smooth. Add the milk and whisk until combined. Set the cream cheese mixture aside.

4. Add the egg whites and cream of tartar to a large, clean bowl.

5. Whisk with electric beaters or a stand mixer on low speed for about 30 seconds, then increase to medium speed. When the egg whites are frothy, start adding the sugar a tablespoon at a time. Continue whisking until stiff peaks form.

6. Add about a quarter of the egg white mixture to the cream cheese mixture and fold it through until combined. Add another quarter and fold it through again very gently. Repeat once more.

7. When only about a quarter of the egg white mixture remains, tip the cream cheese mixture into the bowl with the egg whites and carefully combine.

8. Try to remove any pockets of egg white while maintaining as much air and volume in the batter as possible. Pour the batter into the prepared cake tin. Smooth out the surface of the batter to be as even as possible.

9. To remove any large air bubbles, insert a long wooden skewer into the batter and move it in small concentric circles all around the cake tin. Then lift the tin about 1 cm (½ in) off the kitchen bench and drop it back down three or four times.

10. Place the cake tin in a deep baking dish and fill the outer dish with boiling water until it comes about a third of the way up the side of the round cake tin.

11. Place in the centre of the oven and bake for 1 hour and 45 minutes.

12. Increase the heat to 150°C (300°F) and add more boiling water to the outer baking dish as most of it will have evaporated. Bake for a further 22–24 minutes, at which point the top of the cake should be a light and even golden brown. Remove the cake tin from the oven and set on a cooling rack for 30–40 minutes.

13. Gently turn the cake over and remove the cake tin and the bottom layer of baking paper.

14. Carefully turn the cake the right way up onto a serving plate and slowly peel away the baking paper on its sides. Place the cake in the fridge to cool completely before serving.

Sweet Tart Pastry Dough

Makes enough for 2–3 large tarts or about 40 small tarts

This pastry is not very flaky but much more akin to a shortcrust. It has a very pleasant bite and isn't too crumbly, and best of all, the dough can be rolled very thin. As an added bonus, I created this recipe so that I could *stop* blind-baking, because I find it very tedious. It does benefit from being partially baked before being filled (for example, see the following recipe for my Sticky Date Tart), but there's no need to blink-bake; you simply need to prick the bottom of the tart shell generously before baking. Note that the milk powder in this recipe is optional – mainly because it's usually bought in bulk and I understand that buying a whole bag for one or two recipes isn't ideal. If you plan to bake numerous tarts, however, I'd recommend it as it helps with the pliability of the dough. You also might wonder why this recipe isn't for a single tart shell. It's a larger portion simply because of the whole egg. You can halve this recipe to avoid wastage by halving the egg content. The easiest way to do this is to weigh the egg out of the shell, whisk it lightly, and then discard half the weight of the egg (or save it for an omelette!)

230 g (8 oz) caster (superfine) sugar
115 g (4 oz) butter
1 egg
1 tsp vanilla bean paste
300 g (10 ½ oz) Basic Plain Flour Blend (page 11)
2 tsp milk powder (optional)
1 tsp xanthan gum
¼ tsp salt
1–2 tbsp milk

1. In a large bowl, cream the sugar and butter with electric beaters or the whisk attachment of your stand mixer.

2. Add the egg and vanilla and beat again until combined.

3. Sift together the dry ingredients, then add them to the bowl. If using a stand mixer, swap to the paddle attachment, then mix slowly to incorporate the dry ingredients with the egg and butter mixture. If you don't have a stand mixer, bring the dough together with a spatula and then knead by hand.

4. As the dough forms, increase the speed to medium until the dough is soft and smooth. This will likely take 4–5 minutes with a stand mixer or around 10 minutes by hand.

5. When the dough is ready, divide it in two and wrap each portion in plastic wrap. Place in the fridge for at least 30 minutes.

6. When ready to use, remove the portion(s) needed for the recipe, break it into small pieces and place back in your stand mixer fitted with the paddle attachment (you can also do this by hand on a clean work surface). Add one tablespoon of milk and then mix on medium speed until the dough comes back together and is soft and pliable. You may need to add the second tablespoon of milk if working with both portions of dough.

7. The dough will still be quite cold, but it will be flexible and easy to work with. It is now ready to be rolled and cooked according to the instructions in the tart recipes to follow.

8. If you only need one portion of dough, keep the other sealed well in the fridge where it will keep for five or six days. You can also freeze the unused dough. Thaw it completely in the fridge before using and refer to step 6.

Sticky Date Tart

Serves 8–10

SOY FREE   VEGETARIAN

This tart is an absolute showstopper. Inspired by a sticky date pudding, the nostalgic flavors of dates and butterscotch are elevated at every point by techniques and textures that take the dish up a notch. It is crisp but chewy, sweet but salty and ultimately decadent at every turn. It is a labour of love with different elements that take time to cook or set, but none of the techniques involved are particularly difficult, and it is definitely well worth the effort.

You might not have come across caramelized white chocolate (also known as 'gold' or 'golden' chocolate). While it has been used in desserts and pastries for a long time, it has been popularized over the last few years – at least in Australia – by Cadbury's release of Caramilk chocolate. You can buy caramelized white chocolate chips for cooking, but snack bar varieties work just as well. If you can't find it at all, there are myriad recipes online for making your own from regular white chocolate, or you can leave the ganache off entirely – this tart will still be delicious!

Tart shell

1 portion of Sweet Tart Pastry Dough (page 195)
rice flour, to dust

Sticky date tart filling

30 g (1 oz) pitted dates
60 g (2 oz) soft brown sugar
60 g (2 oz) butter
1 egg
½ tsp vanilla bean paste
60 g (2 oz) almond meal
10 g (¼ oz) Basic Plain Flour Blend (page 11)
¼ tsp GF baking powder
⅛ tsp salt
45 g (1 ½ oz) pitted dates, extra

Salted caramel layer

100 g (3 ½ oz) caster (superfine) sugar
4 tsp water
55 ml (1 ¾ fl oz) single cream
20 g (¾ oz) butter
½ tsp salt flakes

Caramelized white chocolate ganache

140 g (5 oz) caramelized white chocolate, chopped
40 ml (1 ¼ fl oz) single cream

Honey-roasted pecans

50 g (1 ¾ oz) honey
20 g (¾ oz) caster (superfine) sugar
100 g (3 ½ oz) pecans

Tart shell

1. Preheat your oven to 160°C (320°F) and lightly grease a 40 x 14 cm (16 x 5 in) rectangular tart tin.

2. Lightly dust your work surface and rolling pin with rice flour. Roll the dough out into a rectangular shape slightly larger than the tin, ensuring it is approximately 2–3 mm thick.

3. Transfer the dough to your prepared tin by lightly dusting the rolled dough with rice flour and rolling it gently onto your rolling pin. Lift the rolling pin to one end of the tart tin, then carefully unroll the dough towards the other end of the tin. Gently maneuver the dough into the tart tin, filling in the corners and pressing the dough to the walls of the tin. Trim off excess dough with a paring knife by running it horizontally around the rim of the tart tin.

4. Prick the base of the dough generously with a fork, then place on a baking tray in the oven and bake for 14–16 minutes or until the tart shell has turned pale gold in color. The pastry shouldn't rise but some small air bubbles may appear in the base if it wasn't pricked generously enough prior to baking. This isn't a problem – just gently press the pastry back down with the back of a spoon while it is still hot.

5. Leave the tart shell in the tin to cool on a wire rack for 10–15 minutes while you work on the filling.

→

←

Sticky date tart filling

1. Place 30 g (1 oz) of pitted dates in a small bowl and cover with boiling water. Allow to sit for 5–10 minutes.

2. Meanwhile, combine the brown sugar and butter in a food processor and blitz until light and creamy. Add the egg, vanilla and soaked dates (discard the soaking water) and blitz until combined. Add the almond meal, flour, baking powder and salt, then blitz again until smooth.

3. Finely chop the extra 45 g (1½ oz) of pitted dates and fold them through the almond mixture. Spoon the mixture into the semi-baked pastry shell, smooth it out with a palette knife or spatula and bake for 20–25 minutes or until a skewer inserted gently into the filling layer comes out clean. While you wait, prepare the salted caramel.

Salted caramel

1. Place the sugar and water into a medium saucepan over medium-low heat. Stir it gently just to ensure that the sugar is all wetted.

2. Allow it to simmer untouched for 6–8 minutes. It will come to a rapid boil and start to thicken.

3. Heat the cream in the microwave for 30–45 seconds. When the sugar mixture has reached a golden caramel color, remove from heat and carefully add the hot cream, whisking to combine. Be very careful as this will bubble and release a lot of steam.

4. When the cream has been fully incorporated, add the butter and whisk until melted.

5. Season with the salt flakes and set aside to cool for approximately 10 minutes.

6. Pour the cooled salted caramel over the sticky date layer of the tart while the tart is still warm, then allow to set in the fridge for approximately 1 hour.

Caramelized white chocolate ganache

1. To make the caramelized white chocolate ganache, combine the chocolate and cream in a medium microwave-safe bowl. Microwave in 30-second increments, stirring each time, until the chocolate is completely melted.

2. While the ganache is warm but not hot, tip it over the cooled and set salted-caramel layer, then smooth it out using a small offset palette knife or spatula. Place the tart back in the fridge to set the ganache while you make the honey-roasted nuts.

Honey-roasted pecans

1. Preheat your oven to 170°C (340°F) and line a baking tray with parchment paper.

2. Heat the honey and sugar in a medium saucepan over low heat until the sugar has dissolved. Remove from the heat, add the pecans and toss gently until all the nuts are coated in the honey mixture.

3. Turn the nuts out onto the prepared baking tray and bake for 14 minutes, turning the nuts halfway through cooking.

4. Allow the nuts to cool completely on the baking tray. Once cooled, chop the nuts if desired, and arrange them on top of the tart.

5. Keep the finished tart in the fridge, but remove half an hour prior to serving. The tart can be stored in an airtight container in the fridge for three or four days.

Apple Frangipane Tart

Serves 6–8

This tart is deceptively simple, despite how pretty it looks with the apple rose. Don't worry too much about perfecting that, though – the tart will be delicious regardless of the apple configuration!

1 portion of Sweet Tart Pastry Dough (page 195)
rice flour, to dust

Almond frangipane filling

60 g (2 oz) caster (superfine) sugar
60 g (2 oz) butter
1 egg
½ tsp vanilla bean paste
60 g (2 oz) almond meal
10 g (¼ oz) Basic Plain Flour Blend (page 11)
¼ tsp GF baking powder
⅛ tsp salt

Apple garnish

2 ripe apples (I like to use pink lady, granny smith or gala varieties)
½ tsp cinnamon, to dust (optional)
dollop cream, to serve

1. Start by making the tart shell. Preheat oven to 160°C (320°F) and lightly grease a round tart tin, ring or pie dish (approximately 20 cm or 8 in in diameter).

2. Lightly dust your work surface and rolling pin with rice flour. Roll the dough out into a circular shape slightly larger than the tin, ensuring it is approximately 2–3 mm thick.

3. Transfer the dough to your prepared tin by lightly dusting the rolled dough with rice flour and rolling it gently onto your rolling pin. Lift the rolling pin to one end of the tart tin, then carefully unroll the dough towards the other end of the tin. Gently maneuver the dough into the tart tin, filling in the edges and pressing the dough to the walls of the tin. Trim off excess dough with a paring knife by running it horizontally around the rim of the tart tin.

4. Prick the base of the dough generously with a fork, then place on a baking tray in the oven and bake for 14–16 minutes or until the tart shell has turned pale gold in color. The pastry shouldn't rise but some small air bubbles may appear in the base if it wasn't pricked generously enough prior to baking. This isn't a problem – just gently press the pastry back down with the back of a spoon while it is still hot.

5. Once the tart shell has had its first partial bake, leave the tart shell in the tin to cool on a wire rack for 10–15 minutes, then refrigerate it for around 20 minutes.

6. While you're waiting, prepare the almond frangipane filling and apple garnish. In a medium bowl, whisk the sugar and butter with an electric mixer until pale and creamy. Add the egg and vanilla and whisk again until smooth.

→

7. Sift together the dry ingredients and then fold them through the egg and butter mixture until well combined. Set aside.

8. To prepare the apples for the top of the tart, start by making two cuts straight down the apple on either side of the core. This will give you two 'cheeks'.

9. Placing the cheeks flat side down on your chopping board, slice the apples very finely to create lots of semicircular pieces. These pieces should range from 1 mm thickness to about 3 mm thickness. Cut off the partial 'cheeks' left on the core of the apples and repeat the slicing process.

10. Spoon the almond mixture into the cooled tart shell, then spread it with a palette knife or spatula to ensure an even layer of frangipane.

11. To arrange the apples on the tart, ensure that the frangipane is spread smoothly all over the tart base. Starting from the edge of the tart, begin layering in the apple pieces, pressing the flat edges into the frangipane. Overlap the slices slightly and work your way around the edge of the entire tart, then continue layering the apples in a concentric circular pattern. Use thicker slices of apple towards the edge of the tart and thinner slices as you move into the centre as these are more easily bent to accommodate the tighter circular pattern.

12. When the apple 'rose' is complete, dust with cinnamon if you wish, then bake again at 160°C (320°F) for 30–35 minutes or until the apples are cooked and the frangipane filling is set. Allow to cool completely on a wire rack, then serve with dollop cream.

Fig and Pistachio Tarts

Makes 12

Fig and pistachio go together *perfectly*, so these tarts are completely scrumptious. I've added the burnt honey glaze as an optional extra – the tarts are delicious on their own, but the sweetness and caramelisation definitely adds a little something. If you do add the honey, I highly recommend serving these with a spoonful of dollop cream. That takes them from a tasty afternoon tea accompaniment to a fully fledged dessert!

1 portion of Sweet Tart Pastry Dough (page 195)
rice flour, to dust

Pistachio filling

60 g (2 oz) shelled raw pistachios (unsalted)
60 g (2 oz) butter
60 g (2 oz) caster (superfine) sugar
1 egg
1 tsp vanilla bean paste
10 g (¼ oz) Basic Plain Flour Blend (page 11)
¼ tsp GF baking powder
⅛ tsp salt
2–3 fresh figs, sliced into rounds

Burnt honey glaze (optional)

4 tbsp honey
2 tbsp water

1. Start by making the tart shells. Preheat your oven to 160°C (320°F) and lightly grease 12 small fluted tart tins (approximately 8 cm or 3 in in diameter).

2. Lightly dust your work surface and rolling pin with rice flour. Roll the dough out until it is approximately 2–3 mm thick. Using a cookie cutter that is about 12 cm in diameter, cut out 12 circles of pastry.

3. Gently maneuver the pastry circles into the tart tins, filling in the edges and pressing the dough to the walls of the tin. Trim off excess dough with a paring knife by running it horizontally around the rim of the tart tin.

4. Prick the pastry on the base of the tins generously with a fork, then place on a baking tray in the oven and bake for 10–12 minutes or until the tart shells have turned pale gold in color. The pastry shouldn't rise but some small air bubbles may appear in the base of the tarts if they weren't pricked generously enough prior to baking. This isn't a problem – just gently press the pastry back down with the back of a spoon while it is still hot.

5. Leave the tart shells in the tins to cool on a wire rack for 10–15 minutes, then remove them from the tins and refrigerate for around 20 minutes. While you're waiting, prepare the pistachio filling.

6. Blitz the pistachios in a food processor until they are very fine, similar to almond meal. Remove from the processor and set aside.

7. Combine the butter and sugar in the same food processor and blitz until light and creamy. Add the egg and vanilla and process until combined. Add the ground pistachios, flour, baking powder and salt, then blitz again until combined.

8. Spoon or pipe the pistachio filling into the semi-baked pastry shells, filling them up only about a third of the way (the filling will rise in the oven). Add a slice of fig to each tart, pressing it lightly into the pistachio filling.

9. Bake the tarts for 20–25 minutes or until a skewer inserted gently into the filling layer comes out clean.

10. If making the honey glaze, heat the honey in a small saucepan over medium-low heat. When it starts to boil, reduce the heat and let simmer for 4–5 minutes.

11. When the honey has reduced by about two-thirds (it should be dark in color, very thick and sticky), add the water and stir to combine. Remove from the heat and allow the glaze to cool slightly before using a pastry brush to brush the glaze over the finished tarts.

Strawberry Tarts

NUT FREE   SOY FREE   VEGETARIAN

These are a great entry point into tart-making if you haven't made many before. The tart shells can be fiddly if they're very small, so if you're not comfortable trying that, feel free to use a single large tin instead – the combination of creamy custard, crisp pastry and fresh strawberries will be delicious no matter what! If you feel like elevating these a bit, dollop a little homemade or store-bought strawberry jam on the base of the tarts under the custard for an extra fruity mouthful.

1 portion of Sweet Tart Pastry Dough (page 195)
rice flour, to dust
1 egg white and 2 tbsp single cream (whisked together, for egg wash)
3 egg yolks
2 tbsp caster (superfine) sugar
2½ tbsp GF cornstarch
185 ml (6 fl oz) milk
125 ml (4 fl oz) single cream
⅛ tsp salt
1 tsp vanilla bean paste (or extract)
250 g (9 oz) strawberries, quartered

1. Preheat your oven to 160°C (320°F) and line a baking tray with parchment paper. Lightly grease 12 small tart rings of any shape (cook in batches if you have fewer than 12).

2. Lightly dust your work surface and rolling pin with rice flour. Roll the dough out until it is approximately 2–3 mm thick. Use one of the tart rings to cut 12 pieces out of the dough in the same shape as the tart rings – these will become the base of the tart shells. Place the tart rings onto the prepared baking tray and place the cut pastry shapes into them, pressing down gently to compress the pastry snugly into the tart rings.

3. Gather the pastry scraps and knead to bring it back together, then roll it out once more. Cut long strips of pastry, the width corresponding with the height of the sides of the tart rings. Working with one strip at a time, roll it up like a snail shell and transfer it into a tart ring. Place it on its side then unravel it around the inside of the tart ring to form the wall of the tart shell, trimming the pastry where the ends overlap. Remove the scraps.

4. Gently press the pastry into the side of the tart ring (only enough to keep the pastry standing at a right angle to the base – otherwise it will be impossible to remove), then apply pressure along the bottom edge on the inside of the shell to meld the base layer with the sides. Trim off excess dough with a paring knife by running it horizontally around the rim of the tart ring.

→

5. Prick the pastry on the base of the shells generously with a fork, then transfer the baking tray to the oven and bake for 10–12 minutes or until the tart shells have turned pale gold in color. The pastry shouldn't rise but some small air bubbles may appear in the base of the tarts if they weren't pricked generously enough prior to baking. This isn't a problem – just gently press the pastry back down with the back of a spoon while it is still hot.

6. Transfer the tart shells in the rings to a wire rack to cool for 10–15 minutes (use tongs as they'll be too hot to handle), leaving the oven on as they'll be going back in again soon. Once they've cooled slightly, gently push the pastry out of the tart ring by applying pressure on the outer edges at the base of the tart. If the pastry is difficult to remove, it may have been compressed too tightly to the tart ring.

7. Once the shells have been removed from the tart rings, you can neaten the top rims using a microplane or other very fine grater. Hold the pastry flat against the grating surface and lightly glide back and forth to shave the pastry into a neat, straight edge. (This is an optional step and purely for aesthetic purposes.)

8. Use a pastry brush to coat the tart shells with a light layer of the egg wash, brushing the inside and outer sides of the pastry. Place them back on the baking tray and return to the oven for a further 10–12 minutes or until they are a shiny, golden brown color. Once baked, transfer the tart shells to a wire rack to cool completely while you make the filling.

9. Combine the egg yolks, sugar and cornstarch in a medium bowl and whisk until pale and creamy.

10. Heat the milk, cream, salt and vanilla in a medium saucepan until just simmering, stirring constantly with a spatula to prevent the liquid catching on the base of the pan. Slowly pour the hot milk into the egg yolk mixture, whisking briskly and constantly until fully combined. Transfer this custard to a clean saucepan and heat again over low heat, whisking constantly until a thick custard forms.

11. Transfer to a clean bowl and cover with plastic wrap, ensuring that the plastic is directly in contact with the surface of the custard (this prevents a skin forming). Set aside to cool completely.

12. Once the tart shells and custard have both cooled, whisk the custard to ensure it is smooth and transfer to a piping bag. Trim about 1 cm (½ in) off the tip of the bag and fill the tart shells to the brim. Smooth out the top and allow the tarts to set in the fridge for at least an hour before topping them generously with strawberries.

13. Store the finished tarts in an airtight container in the fridge for a day or two. Note that the pastry will soften after prolonged contact with the filling, so if making ahead of time, premake the tart shells and store in an airtight container, then fill before serving.

Chocolate Orange Tarts

Makes 12

Confession: chocolate with orange is not my favorite flavor combination, and I initially only made these at the request of a close friend. But once I made my own orange curd to use as the filling, I was surprised at how much I liked them. It's smooth and rich without being overpowered by acidity, so the orange ends up complementing the chocolate in the best way. For an extra chocolatey kick, top them with the whipped milk-chocolate ganache I use for my Tiramisu Tart (page 213), because you can never have too much chocolate!

1 portion of Sweet Tart Pastry Dough (page 195)

rice flour, to dust

1 egg white and 2 tbsp single cream (whisked together, for egg wash)

3 orange slices cut into quarters, to garnish (optional)

Orange curd filling

2 tbsp orange zest

160 ml (5 ½ fl oz) freshly squeezed orange juice

200 g caster (superfine) sugar

25 g (1 oz) GF cornstarch

¼ tsp salt

6 egg yolks

120 g (4 ½ oz) butter, cubed, at room temperature

Chocolate ganache

100 g (3 ½ oz) milk chocolate, finely chopped

40 ml (1 ¼ fl oz) single cream

1. Start by making the tart shells. Preheat oven to 160°C (320°F) and lightly grease 12 small fluted tart tins (approximately 8 cm or 3 in in diameter).

2. Lightly dust your work surface and rolling pin with rice flour, then roll the dough out until it is approximately 2–3 mm thick. Using a cookie cutter that is about 12 cm (5 in) in diameter, cut out 12 circles of pastry.

3. Gently maneuver the pastry circles into the tart tins, filling in the edges and pressing the dough to the walls of the tin. Trim off excess dough with a paring knife by running it horizontally around the rim of the tart tin.

4. Prick the pastry on the base of the tins generously with a fork, then place on a baking tray in the oven and bake for 10–12 minutes or until the tart shells have turned pale gold in color. The pastry shouldn't rise but some small air bubbles may appear in the base of the tarts if they weren't pricked generously enough prior to baking. This isn't a problem – just gently press the pastry back down with the back of a spoon while it is still hot. Leave the tart shells in the tins to cool on a wire rack for 10–15 minutes, then remove from the tins.

5. Line a baking tray with parchment paper. When the tart shells are cool enough to handle, brush them gently all over with the egg wash. Place on the baking tray and bake for a further 10–15 minutes until they are shiny and a rich golden color. Allow to cool completely on a wire rack.

6. To make the orange curd, prepare a double boiler. In a heatproof bowl off the heat, add all ingredients except the butter and whisk well to combine.

→

7. Place the bowl on the heat and whisk constantly for 6–7 minutes or until the curd has thickened significantly. There should be no floury taste, so if this persists, cook a little longer, ensuring you're whisking constantly.

8. When you can no longer discern the floury taste, add the butter bit by bit, whisking after each addition until fully melted and incorporated. Transfer the finished curd into a fresh bowl or container and cover with plastic wrap, ensuring that the plastic is directly in contact with all of the exposed curd (this prevents a skin forming on the surface). Place in the fridge to cool for at least 30 minutes.

9. When the curd is sufficiently cool (it should have thickened further), spoon or pipe it into the prepared tart shells, only filling them about two-thirds of the way. Smooth the curd to create an even surface area, then refrigerate the tarts for another 30 minutes.

10. To make the chocolate ganache, place the chocolate and cream in a microwave-safe bowl. Heat in 30-second increments (stirring after each time) until the chocolate has melted into the cream. Mix well to ensure it is smooth.

11. Allow the ganache to cool slightly (it should not be too hot to touch), then pour evenly over the curd in the tart shells, filling the shells up completely. Refrigerate again until completely cooled – this will solidify the ganache.

12. Garnish with orange slices if desired and serve.

Tiramisu Tart

Serves 8–10

This is another tart that is *delicious* but not for the faint-hearted. Don't get me wrong: none of the elements are especially difficult to make, but there are definitely more steps than you might be used to, and as such, it's quite time-consuming. Some of the elements need to be made ahead, so be sure to read the recipe before you get started. I'd suggest you work your way up to this tart by trying some of the simpler ones, or take it on when you're keen to challenge yourself with a weekend project. Rest assured that the effort *will* be worth it!

Whipped milk-chocolate ganache

- 20 ml (¾ fl oz) water
- 5 g (⅛ oz) powdered gelatine
- 500 g (1 lb 2 oz) whipping or double cream
- 200 g (7 oz) milk chocolate, chopped

Mascarpone cream topping

- 500 ml (17 fl oz) whipping or double cream
- 30 g (1 oz) GF icing sugar
- 1 tsp vanilla bean paste (or extract)
- 125 g (4 fl oz) mascarpone

Tart shell

- 1 portion of Sweet Tart Pastry Dough (page 195)
- rice flour, to dust

Dark chocolate ganache

- 80 ml (2 ½ fl oz) single cream
- ½ tsp instant coffee granules
- 80 g (2 ¾ oz) dark chocolate, finely chopped

Sponge cake layer

- 2 eggs (about 100 g or 3 ½ oz)
- 60 g (2 oz) caster (superfine) sugar
- 55 g (2 oz) Basic Plain Flour Blend (page 11)
- ½ tsp GF baking powder
- ½ tsp vanilla bean paste (or extract)
- 40 ml (1 ¼ fl oz) espresso coffee (or equivalent using instant coffee)

Assembly

- 1 ½ tbsp cocoa powder
- coffee beans, to decorate (optional)

Whipped milk-chocolate ganache

1. The whipped ganache must be made in advance as it needs to cool and set completely before assembly (5–6 hours). Place the water in a small bowl and sprinkle the gelatine over the surface. Set aside.

2. In a medium saucepan, add the cream and bring to a simmer over medium-low heat, stirring occasionally with a spatula. Place the chopped chocolate in a deep bowl and add the bloomed gelatine. Pour the hot cream over the chocolate and gelatine and let sit for about a minute.

3. Blend the chocolate and cream mixture with a stick blender or by stirring vigorously with a spatula until completely smooth and homogenous. Pour the ganache into a bowl or container, cover with plastic wrap so that the plastic is in contact with the entire surface of the ganache to avoid a skin forming, and place in the fridge to cool completely and set for 5–6 hours.

Mascarpone cream topping

1. The mascarpone cream topping must also be made in advance. On a sheet of baking paper, use a plate or bowl to trace a circle that is approximately 24 cm (9 in) in diameter (or a few centimetres smaller than the tart tin you're using). Place the baking paper drawn side down on a baking tray and set aside.

2. Add all ingredients to the bowl of a stand mixer fitted with a whisk attachment or a large mixing bowl. Whisk with an electric mixer at low speed until the ingredients are combined, then increase to medium speed.

→

3. Whisk until stiff peaks have formed, then transfer the cream mixture to a piping bag fitted with a teardrop or St Honore piping tip. Alternatively, you can use scissors to make a similar shape by cutting off the tip of the piping bag at a sharp angle. Pipe the cream mixture in condensed random swirls onto the lined baking paper, making sure the cream goes beyond the edges of the circle that you traced (the excess will be trimmed).

4. Place the baking tray with the piped cream mixture into the freezer for 2–3 hours.

Tart shell

1. To make the tart shell, preheat oven to 160°C (320°F) and lightly grease a large round tart tin (approximately 28 cm or 11 in in diameter).

2. Lightly dust your work surface and rolling pin with rice flour. Roll the dough out into a circular shape slightly larger than the tin, ensuring it is approximately 2–3 mm thick.

3. Transfer the dough to your prepared tin by lightly dusting the rolled dough with rice flour and rolling it gently onto your rolling pin. Lift the rolling pin to one end of the tart tin, then carefully unroll the dough towards the other end of the tin. Gently maneuver the dough into the tart tin, filling in the edges and pressing the dough to the walls of the tin. Trim off excess dough with a paring knife by running it horizontally around the rim of the tart tin.

4. Prick the base of the dough generously with a fork, then place on a baking tray in the oven and bake for 14–16 minutes or until the tart shell has turned pale gold in color. The pastry shouldn't rise but some small air bubbles may appear in the base if it wasn't pricked generously enough prior to baking. This isn't a problem – just gently press the pastry back down with the back of a spoon while it is still hot. Leave the tart shell in the tin to cool on a wire rack for 10–15 minutes, then remove it from the tin and refrigerate for around 20 minutes. While you're waiting, prepare the dark chocolate ganache.

Dark chocolate ganache

1. Put the cream in a small microwave-safe bowl and microwave for 30–40 seconds. Add the coffee granules and whisk until the coffee has dissolved. You may need to reheat the cream slightly.

2. Add the chopped dark chocolate to the coffee cream mixture and microwave for another 30 seconds. Whisk until the mixture is smooth. Pour the ganache into the cooled tart shell and gently tip and swirl it so that the ganache evenly coats the base of the tart. Smooth it out with a palette knife or spatula if necessary. Place it back in the fridge to set while you work on the cake filling.

Sponge cake layer

1. Preheat oven to 160°C (320°F) and grease and line a 30 x 20 cm (12 x 8 in) baking tray.

2. Prepare a double boiler, then add the eggs and sugar to a large heatproof mixing bowl. Place the bowl over the heat, whisking constantly until the sugar has dissolved. This will happen at about 50°C (120°F) if you have a thermometer, but you can also test by rubbing the mixture between your thumb and forefinger to see if you can feel sugar granules.

3. Remove the bowl from the heat then whisk using electric beaters or a stand mixer until it reaches the ribbon stage: this is when you can stop the whisk and, if you lift it out of the bowl, the mixture will stream off it in a thick, glossy ribbon, pooling gently in the bowl. This should take around 4–6 minutes of whisking on high speed.

4. Sift in the flour and baking powder, add the vanilla and fold gently with a spatula to combine, removing any lumps while trying to maintain as much air and volume as possible.

5. Pour the batter into the lined baking tray and smooth to create an even layer. Bake for 15–18 minutes until the sponge is golden on top and springs back when touched. Turn the cake out onto a cooling rack.

6. To assemble, remove the tart shell with the base layer of ganache from the fridge. You will now need a layer of sponge slightly smaller than the tart shell. The easiest way to do this will be to cut two semicircular shapes, back to back, from the long edges of the cake. Then cut a long, thin rectangle from the short edge of the remaining sponge and use this to fill the gap between the semicircles to form a nearly perfect circle of sponge. Assemble this on top of the ganache in the tart shell. Don't worry too much about the sponge fitting neatly into the shell. You can use smaller pieces of sponge to fill any gaps.

7. Brush the sponge circle liberally with the espresso using a pastry brush.

Assembly

1. Remove the whipped milk-chocolate ganache from the fridge and add it to the bowl of a stand mixer (alternatively, use electric beaters). Whip the ganache on medium-high speed until stiff peaks form. It should resemble a very creamy and thick mousse.

2. Spoon or pipe the whipped ganache into the tart, covering the sponge and filling in the gap between the sponge and the tart shell. Push down gently as you smooth it out to remove any air pockets in the tart. When the whipped ganache is as smooth on the surface as possible (it should completely fill your tart shell), dust the outer edge with the cocoa powder using a small sieve.

3. Remove the piped mascarpone cream from the freezer. Using the plate or bowl you traced the circle on the baking paper with as a guide, cut out the circle of topping. This will be made easier by heating a knife in very hot water before wiping it dry and slicing. Using a palette knife or flat spatula, carefully lift the circle of frozen cream topping onto the tart, being careful to centre it as best as you can.

4. Decorate with coffee beans if desired, then leave the tart in the fridge until ready to serve (it's best taken out two or three hours before serving as the mascarpone cream will then thaw but retain its shape). The tart can also sit at room temperature for up to two hours.

Lemon Meringue Tarts

Makes 12

If you love lemon meringue pie, you're bound to adore these smaller versions. The curd is sharp but sweet, and the Swiss meringue on top is somehow airy and creamy at the same time. I've taken these to many gatherings of friends and family, and they always go down an absolute treat. The only problem is that you'll then be asked to bring them to every event!

Note that you can make the tart shells and curd ahead of time. Once cooled, the tart shells can be stored in an airtight container for four or five days. The curd can be stored in the fridge. The meringue should be used immediately after whipping, but the finished tarts (with the meringue piped *and* torched) can be stored in the fridge for two or three days.

1 portion of Sweet Tart Pastry Dough (page 195)
rice flour, to dust
1 egg white and 2 tbsp single cream (whisked together, for egg wash)

Lemon curd

125 ml (4 fl oz) lemon juice
2 tbsp lemon zest
6 egg yolks
20 g (¾ oz) GF cornstarch
230 g (8 oz) caster (superfine) sugar
130 g (4½ oz) unsalted butter, cubed (at room temperature)
⅛ tsp salt

Swiss meringue

3 egg whites (about 110 g or 4 oz)
110 g (4 oz) caster (superfine) sugar
⅛ tsp cream of tartar
1 tsp vanilla bean paste (or extract)

1. Preheat oven to 160°C (320°F) and lightly grease 12 small fluted tart tins (approximately 8 cm or 3 in in diameter).

2. Lightly dust your work surface and rolling pin with rice flour. Roll the dough out until it is approximately 2–3 mm thick. Using a cookie cutter that is about 12 cm (5 in) in diameter, cut out 12 pastry circles.

3. Gently maneuver the pastry circles into the tart tins, filling in the edges and pressing the dough to the walls of the tin. Trim off excess dough with a paring knife by running it horizontally around the rim of the tart tin.

4. Prick the pastry on the base of the tins generously with a fork, then place on a baking tray in the oven and bake for 10–12 minutes or until the tart shells have turned pale gold in color. The pastry shouldn't rise but some small air bubbles may appear in the base of the tarts if they weren't pricked generously enough prior to baking. This isn't a problem – just gently press the pastry back down with the back of a spoon while it is still hot. Leave the tart shells in the tins to cool on a wire rack for 10–15 minutes, then remove from the tins.

5. Line a baking tray with parchment paper. When the tart shells are cool enough to handle, brush them gently all over with the egg wash. Place on the baking tray and bake for a further 10–15 minutes, until they are shiny and a rich golden color. Allow to cool completely on a wire rack.

→

6. To make the curd, prepare a double boiler. Place all ingredients except the butter and salt into a large heatproof mixing bowl. Whisk well to combine then place it over the heat, whisking constantly. As it heats, the curd will start to thicken.

7. When the curd is the consistency of thick custard, start adding the butter one cube at a time, whisking constantly to incorporate. When all the butter has been mixed in, the curd should be smooth, thick and glossy. Remove it from the heat and season with the salt.

8. Pour the curd through a sieve into a bowl to cool, covering it with plastic wrap so that the plastic sits directly on the curd's surface to prevent a skin from forming.

9. When the curd and tart shells have cooled, mix the curd well with a spatula and spoon or pipe it into the tart shells. Overfill them slightly, then use a palette knife or the flat edge of a butter knife to scrape off the excess and create a perfectly flat surface on which to pipe the meringue. When all the tarts are filled, place them in the fridge to set for at least 30 minutes before you start making the meringue.

10. To make the Swiss meringue, prepare a double boiler, then place the egg whites, sugar and cream of tartar in a large bowl or the bowl of your stand mixer. Whisk briefly with a handheld whisk to combine. Place the bowl over the heat and whisk constantly until the sugar has dissolved and the temperature of the egg whites reaches 60°C (140°F).

11. Remove the bowl from the heat and start whisking with an electric whisk, beater or a stand mixer fitted with a whisk attachment. Start on low to medium speed for about a minute, then increase to high speed.

12. Whisk until medium peaks form (the meringue should be very thick and glossy), then add the vanilla and continue whisking on high speed. When the meringue holds stiff peaks (this can take a total of 10–15 minutes, depending on your mixer), stop whisking and use a spatula to smooth the surface of the meringue.

13. Remove the tarts from the fridge then, one at a time, dip the tarts into the meringue. Do this by holding the base of the pastry firmly, then turn the tart curd side down and lower it into the meringue so that just the surface of the tart is submerged. Bring it out smoothly so that the meringue holds onto the tart until it is pulled away, forming a neat peak. Alternatively, you can use a piping bag to pipe the meringue onto each tart. As each tart is dipped, ensure that the surface of the meringue is still relatively flat, smoothing with a spatula as necessary.

14. Once all the tarts have been topped, use a brûlée torch to lightly brown the meringue. They will burn easily, so start by holding the torch a good distance from the meringue and move closer as you gauge the strength of the flame.

15. Once lightly torched, the tarts are ready to serve straight away.

Lime and Ginger Meringue Tarts

Makes 12

I know some people might be reluctant to try this spin on the classic lemon meringue but I *promise* you won't be sorry. These have all the good bits of a lemon meringue – the balance of sweet and tart flavors along with the mellow meringue – but also have a warmth from the ginger in the curd that makes it very hard not to keep going back for more!

Note that you can make the tart shells and curd ahead of time. Once cooled, the tart shells can be stored in an airtight container for four or five days. The curd can be stored in the fridge. The meringue should be piped immediately after whipping, but the finished tarts (with the meringue piped *and* torched) can be stored in the fridge for two or three days.

---

1 portion of Sweet Tart Pastry Dough (page 195)
rice flour, to dust
1 egg white and 2 tbsp single cream (whisked together, for egg wash)
1–2 tsp lime zest, to garnish

Lime and ginger curd

125 ml (4 fl oz) lime juice
2 tbsp lime zest
6 egg yolks
20 g (¾ oz) GF cornstarch
230 g (8 oz) caster (superfine) sugar
50 g (1 ¾ oz) ginger, finely grated (with the juice)
130 g (4 ½ oz) unsalted butter, cubed (at room temperature)
⅛ tsp salt

Swiss meringue

3 egg whites (about 110 g or 4 oz)
110 g (4 oz) caster (superfine) sugar
⅛ tsp cream of tartar
1 tsp vanilla bean paste (or extract)

1. Preheat oven to 160°C (320°F) and lightly grease 12 small fluted tart tins (approximately 8 cm or 3 in in diameter).

2. Lightly dust your work surface and rolling pin with rice flour. Roll the dough out until it is approximately 2–3 mm thick. Using a cookie cutter that is about 12 cm (5 in) in diameter, cut out 12 pastry circles.

3. Gently maneuver the pastry circles into the tart tins, filling in the edges and pressing the dough to the walls of the tin. Trim off excess dough with a paring knife by running it horizontally around the rim of the tart tin.

4. Prick the pastry on the base of the tins generously with a fork, then place on a baking tray in the oven and bake for 10–12 minutes or until the tart shells have turned pale gold in color. The pastry shouldn't rise but some small air bubbles may appear in the base of the tarts if they weren't pricked generously enough prior to baking. This isn't a problem – just gently press the pastry back down with the back of a spoon while it is still hot. Leave the tart shells in the tins to cool on a wire rack for 10–15 minutes, then remove from the tins.

5. Line a baking tray with parchment paper. When the tart shells are cool enough to handle, brush them gently all over with the egg wash. Place on the baking tray and bake for a further 10–15 minutes, until they are shiny and a rich golden color. Allow to cool completely on a wire rack.

→

6. To make the curd, prepare a double boiler and place all ingredients except the butter and salt into a large heatproof bowl. Whisk to combine, then place it over the heat, whisking constantly. As it heats, the curd will start to thicken.

7. When the curd is the consistency of thick custard, start adding the butter one cube at a time, whisking constantly to incorporate. When all the butter has been mixed in, the curd should be smooth, thick and glossy. Remove it from the heat and season it with the salt.

8. Pour the curd through a sieve into a bowl to cool, covering it with plastic wrap so that the plastic sits directly on the curd's surface to prevent a skin from forming.

9. When the curd and tart shells have cooled, mix the curd well with a spatula and spoon or pipe it into the tart shells. Overfill them slightly, then use a palette knife or the flat edge of a butter knife to scrape off the excess and create a perfectly flat surface on which to pipe the meringue. When all the tarts are filled, place them in the fridge to set the curd while you make the meringue.

10. Prepare a double boiler, then place the egg whites, sugar and cream of tartar in a large heatproof bowl or the bowl of your stand mixer. Whisk briefly with a handheld whisk to combine. Place the bowl over the heat and whisk constantly until the sugar has dissolved and the temperature of the egg whites reaches 60°C (140°F).

11. Remove the bowl from the heat and start whisking with an electric whisk, beater or a stand mixer fitted with a whisk attachment. Start on low to medium speed for about a minute, then increase to high speed.

12. Whisk until medium peaks form (the meringue should be very thick and glossy), then add the vanilla and continue whisking on high speed.

13. When the meringue holds stiff peaks (this can take a total of 10–15 minutes, depending on your mixer), stop whisking and transfer the meringue to a piping bag. Remove the tarts from the fridge.

14. To achieve the effect pictured, simply cut off about 2 cm (¾ in) from the tip of the piping bag to form a round hole, then pipe a generous blob of meringue on one side of a tart. Use a palette knife or the back of a spoon to press down the top of the blob and smear to the opposite side of the tart. Do one tart at a time to prevent the meringue from setting atop the tart before you smear it as this will create some small cracks in the meringue (which won't affect the taste but will be noticeable when torched).

15. Once all the tarts have been topped, use a brûlée torch to lightly brown the meringue. (They will burn easily, so start by holding the torch a good distance from the meringue and move closer as you gauge the strength of the flame.)

16. Sprinkle the tarts with a little lime zest for a final pop of color.

Almond, Pear and Brown Sugar Tart

Serves 8–10

SOY FREE VEGETARIAN

This tart is rich and sweet, and while it's great all year round, using in-season pears really takes it up a notch. As it's quite large, it's the perfect tart to take somewhere when you've been tasked with bringing dessert. Serve it with some ice cream or cream and it'll be a total winner.

1 portion of Sweet Tart Pastry Dough (page 195)
rice flour, to dust
GF icing sugar, to dust
vanilla ice cream or dollop cream, to serve

Filling

120 g (4 ½ oz) soft brown sugar
120 g (4 ½ oz) butter
2 eggs
1 tsp vanilla bean paste
120 g (4 ½ oz) almond meal
20 g (¾ oz) Basic Plain Flour Blend (page 11)
½ tsp GF baking powder
¼ tsp salt
3–4 pears
100 g (3 ½ oz) flaked almonds

1. Preheat oven to 160°C (320°F) and lightly grease a large round tart tin (approximately 28 cm or 11 in in diameter).

2. Lightly dust your work surface and rolling pin with rice flour. Roll the dough out into a circular shape slightly larger than the tin, ensuring it is approximately 2–3 mm thick.

3. Transfer the dough to your prepared tin by lightly dusting the rolled dough with rice flour and rolling it gently onto your rolling pin. Lift the rolling pin to one end of the tart tin, then carefully unroll the dough towards the other end of the tin. Gently maneuver the dough into the tart tin, filling in the edges and pressing the dough to the walls of the tin. Trim off excess dough with a paring knife by running it horizontally around the rim of the tart tin.

4. Prick the base of the dough generously with a fork, then place on a baking tray in the oven and bake for 14–16 minutes or until the tart shell has turned pale gold in color. The pastry shouldn't rise but some small air bubbles may appear in the base if it wasn't pricked generously enough prior to baking. This isn't a problem – just gently press the pastry back down with the back of a spoon while it is still hot.

5. Leave the tart shell in the tin to cool on a wire rack for 10–15 minutes, then remove it from the tin and refrigerate for around 20 minutes. While you're waiting, prepare the filling. If you're going to be filling the tart straight away after it has cooled, you might want to leave your oven on.

6. In a medium bowl, whisk the sugar and butter with an electric mixer until creamy. Add the eggs and vanilla and whisk again until smooth.

7. Sift together the almond meal, flour, baking powder and salt and then fold this through the egg and butter mixture until well combined. Spoon half of this mixture into the cooled tart shell, then spread it with a palette knife or spatula to ensure an even layer of frangipane.

8. Halve and core the pears then place them facedown into the filling, pressing them in gently. Depending on the size of the pears, 6–8 halves should fit in the tart shell. Use a spoon or piping bag to distribute the remaining filling around the pears. Sprinkle the flaked almonds all over the top of the tart, largely avoiding the pears.

9. Place the tart back in the oven (160°C or 320°F) for 45–50 minutes or until the filling is set, the pears are cooked, and the pastry is golden brown.

10. Allow to cool slightly before removing the tart from the tin and dusting with icing sugar. Serve warm or cold with ice cream or dollop cream as desired.

Acknowledgements

There are many people I need to thank for their contribution in bringing this book together.

Primarily, thanks to my endlessly patient and supportive partner. Thank you for being my sounding board and taste tester, my critic and my best friend. I can't articulate how much I appreciate that you never complained about the mess I made in the kitchen while perfecting dozens of recipes. You also deserve a very special mention for being my hand model for many of the pictures in the book.

To my parents – thanks, Mum, for inspiring me to be in the kitchen from such a young age. You instilled in me a love and curiosity for food that is a huge part of who I am. On the flip side, Dad, I love you but we both know that the most you taught me about food was how *not* to cook. Which I still very much appreciate!

Thanks also to the wonderful friends who ate the leftovers from my many cooking endeavours, whether they were successful or not. I truly appreciate all the feedback – the positive, the constructive and everything in between. You've helped to make sure that my recipes are being held to the standard expected of food containing gluten, which I certainly couldn't have done alone!

To Armelle and the team at Affirm – thank you for taking a chance on me. Putting a cookbook together has been a dream of mine since I was five or six years old. I still have the scrapbook of random recipes I cut and pasted from magazines. To think that tatty old plastic folder has manifested into a real book that I can hold and share with my friends and family is quite overwhelming. Thanks also to Simon from Hardie Grant for helping to bring this book to the gluten-free community outside of Australia. This has been a wonderful development that I'm so excited about – I really hope that it can bring back the joy in food for many more people for a long time to come.

I have to sincerely thank my PhD supervisor, Sue, for understanding when I needed some breathing room from my research. There were plenty of days when I thought that trying to write a cookbook and thesis at the same time was utter madness, but your patience and encouragement helped to keep the finish line in mind and stopped me from throwing in the towel. I promise not to try to write any other books until after I graduate!

Finally, thank you to my *MasterChef* family. I learned so much from you all and going through that experience cemented some amazing friendships. You're all a huge part of something that made this book possible so thank you and hopefully see you soon for more endless conversations about food.

Much love to you all,
Mel

About the Author

Melanie Persson was on *MasterChef Australia* 2022 and was the first contestant to compete as a gluten-free cook. Since being diagnosed with celiac disease in 2016, she has worked hard to develop recipes that replicate the foods she used to love. These are largely influenced by her experiences living in Japan and Italy, as well as her Swedish heritage. Mel is passionate about helping people on gluten-free diets rediscover their joy for food and cooking. Whenever she isn't cooking and sharing recipes, she is working on her research as a PhD candidate in the field of children's literature. You can find her on Instagram as @theveryhungrycoeliac.

Index

Published in 2025 by Hardie Grant Books,
an imprint of Hardie Grant Publishing,
by arrangement with Affirm Press

Hardie Grant Books (Melbourne)
Wurundjeri Country
Building 1, 658 Church Street
Richmond, Victoria 3121

Hardie Grant North America
2912 Telegraph Ave
Berkeley, California 94705

hardiegrant.com/books

Hardie Grant acknowledges the Traditional Owners
of the Country on which we work, the Wurundjeri
People of the Kulin Nation and the Gadigal People
of the Eora Nation, and recognises their continuing
connection to the land, waters and culture. We pay
our respects to their Elders past and present.

 A catalogue record for this
book is available from the
National Library of Australia

The Very Hungry Celiac
ISBN 978 1 76145 142 3
ISBN 978 1 76145 143 0 (ebook)

10 9 8 7 6 5 4 3 2 1

Colour reproduction by Splitting Image Cover Studio
Printed in China by Leo Paper Products LTD.

The paper this book is printed on is from FSC®-
certified forests and other sources. FSC® promotes
environmentally responsible, socially beneficial and
economically viable management of the world's forests.